The Flower of Heaven

The Flower of Heaven

Opening the Divine Heart
Through Conscious Friendship
& Love Activism

TARA BIANCA

one love heals all

The Flower of Heaven:
Opening the Divine Heart Through Conscious Friendship &
Love Activism

Published by OneLoveHealsAll Publishing

ISBN: 9780992016111
Printed in the USA

Cover & author photos by © Jarusha Brown|
www.jarushabrown.com

Drawings by Mark Gregory Siermaczeski

Dedicated to you,
a blessing to the world!
I love you. Thank you for being born ;)

If ever there is tomorrow when we're not together…
there is something you must always remember.
You are braver than you believe, stronger than you seem,
and smarter than you think. But the most important thing is,
even if we're apart… I'll always be with you.
~ Winnie the Pooh

Table of Contents

Introduction

I have loved you with an everlasting love;
and I have drawn you with unfailing kindness.
~ Jeremiah 31:3

What is this life about? What is my purpose? Who am I?

There is a great curiosity within you. You are aware of a greater quest within you, an impulse to awaken, to be and to know more, to be a change maker, and to live your purpose.

What is the 'more' that you sense, but cannot seem to put your finger on? You are aware that something has been both beckoning and eluding you. What is that mysterious something?

The mystery leaves you wondering, questioning, and questing. Sometimes you feel unsettled because you know there should be more to your life, but you cannot seem to grasp it. You reflect, maybe if I do 'this' or 'that' I would feel better or be acceptable, or life would be more acceptable in some way.

The mystery has everything to do with your relationship with yourself, the Creator, your friends, family, and the world. Your desire or need for love, acceptance, friendship, and connection are great pointers to the mystery too.

1

Since I was six years old, I have been on the same path as many questers to answer the call to the mystery of me, the mystery of existence, and the mystery of the Divine. I would have liked someone to mentor me or be in community with me on my journey.

From deep aloneness I called out to the lure of the mystery and connected with the Divine as best I could. Since then I have become a finder and have discovered some keys, clues, illuminations, and revelations in relationship with the mystery. Along the way I have encountered others who found their way, too. I honor their service of Love and Truth.

Throughout my journey I have also learned the importance of sharing my spiritual and personal friendship with those in need. I choose to serve others who feel alone and uncertain on the journey, and to mentor those who are ready to know who they are and why they are here. When I was young, I felt lost and alone hoping for a mentor like me. So here I am. I wished myself into being. My longing for connection, love, spiritual mentorship, and answers to the mystery shaped my path and created a solution for me and for others.

Along with other change makers, evolutionary ambassadors, and spiritual visionaries, I am here to declare that life is no longer about the old paradigms of taming, extraction, pollution, and depletion of nature. Nor is it about the prideful ranking of nations or exploitation of people. We are lost when we turn to the consumption of distractions, such as shopping, over-eating, excess entertainment, and addiction to devices. These distractions just deepen disconnection from ourselves, others, nature, and the

Divine. Life is also not about spiritual escapism, elitism, or enlightenment of the few for the benefit of those individuals. Now more than ever those who awaken have the opportunity to serve the world by sharing their wisdom and mentorship.

Awakening and enlightenment are for the world.

The spiritual mystery into awakening is inviting us into a greater relationship with ourselves, others, nature, and with the Divine mystery itself. Rather than awakening in isolation to transcend existence, we are being called to collective awakening to co-create an active, ever-evolving manifestation of Heaven on earth.

Education, entertainment, government, agriculture, medicine, business, spirituality, parenting, and technology will all change. You and I know this. We feel and see the sickness; we know that a new paradigm for healing is required. First, we summon change through our creative vision. We hold the distant star of our vision in our mind and heart. Then we walk the path of change, course-correcting if ever we stray from our goal.

All of life seeks to awaken you. Peacefully rest into the acceptance of the nowness of you and the way things are in the world. At the same time, joyfully hold the seeds of awakening, the seeds of solutions within you. Nurture these seeds letting the beauty of wisdom, compassion, and love blossom. As you share the beauty of you with the world, the world is blessed by your very existence.

As you read let the words in this book nourish you. Allow the energy of the Flower of Heaven to bless and activate you. If you feel confused or challenged by a concept or a chapter, I encourage you to read on. Other parts of the book will inform and shift your understanding. You may find that if you read the book again you will experience it differently and go even deeper into your understanding of it.

The book is written in two parts. Part One offers spiritual insight and revelation into the Flower of Heaven. Part Two presents practical applications, helpful mindsets, and powerful prayers for the teachings in the first part of the book.

There will be many new terms and phrases included in this book. I use them to describe my experiences that would otherwise be indescribable. I will explain as much as I can. However, some words or phrases will become clearer and more meaningful as you continue to read the book. Some words may remain mysterious to you, so I invite you into experiencing them rather than understanding them with your mind.

Some of the phrases I use include *the field*, *the field of existence*, or *the field of creation*. The field is that which is both seen and unseen: the physical, emotional, mental, spiritual, energetic, and etheric. The field can be affected, changed, and influenced by individuals and communities. It is pregnant with possibility and is ever changing. I see it as scaffolding that exists in the now. The field is Divine creation ripe for co-creation with us. When I refer to *the field of Love*, I am referring to Heaven.

I often use the words *embody* or *embodiment*. Embody means to be an expression of an idea, quality, or feeling. To embody love or to be the embodiment of love means to *be* the expression of love through loving thoughts, words, and deeds.

When I capitalize any words that are not normally capitalized, it is to link them with the Divine: Truth, Grace, Love, or Connection. Capitalizing them is a way for me to say… Pay attention, these words have a deeper, sacred meaning.

I am saying… Love is not the love you have most likely learned about while growing up. Ego love is often tied in with condition, suffering, fear, and angst. Divine Love is unconditional and free.

I am saying… Truth is the profound actuality of existence and creation, which supersedes the mind's idea of reality, as the mind is often corrupted by fear and lies.

I am saying… Connection is our Ultimate Reality, as we are ultimately One. Ego connection is the longing we experience when we reside in the lie that we are disconnected.

These can be heavy statements in an introduction. I do not expect people to fully grasp them just yet. Allow yourself to have a sense of the meaning of these statements and let this book take you even deeper into understanding them.

As I share simple, powerful words and concepts about the mystery, I use words like *God*, *Divine*, and *Creator*.

In my youth I avoided using the word *God*, as it had so many connotations from its use in various religious contexts. When speaking with others I worried that people might have negative associations with *God* or their own personal ideas about what *God* represents.

In the last decade I have reclaimed the word *God* releasing any and all negative meanings by letting the love I share with the Creator wash away everything else.

The word *God* is merely a pointer to that which is nameless. The word *God* is synonymous with Divine, Allah, Brahmin, Shiva, Shakti, Tao, Spirit, Universe, Naam, I AM, YHWH, or Creator. What I am pointing to when I use any of these words is 'That Which Created Everything' or 'The Greatest Creator of Existence' or 'The One True Creator of All.' You have your own words to describe or name that which created everything. I honor your words too.

Let me share a little about the words '*I AM*,' as I use them many times to evoke an energy as you read. When I use these words, I am referencing God's holy name or, more specifically, God's holy beingness. In the old testament, God shares with Moses, "*I AM WHO I AM.*" Then the Divine instructs Moses, "*Say this to the people of Israel, 'I AM has sent me to you.'*"[1]

I also reference Christian, Buddhist, Taoist, Sikh, and Vedic writings. As one awakens, spiritual texts reveal a deeper meaning and more clearly point 'the way' home to the Truth of God, the Truth of You. I am a deeply spiritual person who respects religions that create community, actively serve the disenfranchised, and open people to the Love and Truth of the Divine. At the heart of my experience I am in a devoted and loving relationship with the Creator of All. Because we are the creation of the Divine and we are ultimately Divine, I serve God when I serve you. I serve the Truth of Me, but I also serve the Truth of You.

I use the word *God* freely because my relationship with the Divine is deeply personal. There is no real word to name or describe God, as the Divine is indescribable, nameless, and multifaceted everything-ness. Although, if I were to name God, I might use the word *Love*. Let me tell you why…

Love Is

Love is the embodiment of profound acceptance, the recognition of oneself, another, and all of existence, free from the influence of any ideas or beliefs. Love evolves out of the stillness of present moment awareness, yet the state of love is imbued with radiant aliveness. Love is an active power, which exists only in the present moment, free from the past and any ideas of the future; it is a state of being, an experience of loving.

True love exists without the participation of another person; it requires nothing in return, free from the influence of reciprocation. Loving, free of all influence, is the entry point into the freedom state of sovereignty at the level of the soul. When we open to loving, we embody true freedom. From embodiment of love and freedom we are nourished by limitless creative energy, become informed by a greater wisdom, and all action is effortless. The embodiment of love awakens one's consciousness into a profound awareness of Divine Love.

Divine Love exists beyond the mind where all ideas of separation are annihilated, as separation does not and has not ever existed.

Part I - Insight

God is equally present in all creatures;
but all creatures are not equally aware of the fact.
~ Aldous Huxley

Chapter 1 - Inspiration

Only by undistracted love can men see me, and know me,
and enter into me. He who does my work, who loves me,
who sees me as the highest, free from attachment to all things,
and with love for all creation, he in truth comes to me.
~ 11:53-55, Bhagavad Gita

Today a mysterious gift was left at the edge of my awareness. The gift was the revelation of the Flower of Heaven. I was curious, as I had never heard of the Flower of Heaven before today.

I chose to accept and surrender to the Flower of Heaven. When it entered my heart center, the Divine sang through me slowly revealing the wisdom of the Flower of Heaven and the beauty of you. The Divine revealed to me who you are. Knowing who you are I cannot do anything but love you unconditionally.

The revelation and the gift of the Flower of Heaven is for you too.

If you are ready to love you, honor you, be loved and begin waking up to the truth about you, then I am inviting you to awaken to the beauty of you.

Your beauty moves me. My eyes are captivated by the everything of you. The Love of you is forever.

Here, there, and everywhere the Divine loves you. Here, there, and everywhere the invitation to love the Divine sings out. There is nothing you need to do in this lifetime to justify living. There is nothing you need to be. You are loved unconditionally.

God is the dance and the great romance that seeks to awaken you, to reveal you to you.

Your very birth is a blessing for us all. I celebrate the timing and the significance of you coming into my lifetime. You have a unique purpose and path that beautifies existence.

Let yourself resonate with the Truth of these words.

If you are surprised by these statements, your mind may try to convince you it cannot be possible. Throughout most of your life your mind has likely been doing an effective job of telling you that you are not good enough, that you have to be a certain way to be loved, that you should protect yourself from rejection, and that you should worry about what others think about you. And you have been believing these thoughts for a very long time.

It is time to wake up from the lies you have been telling yourself, as the lies block you from knowing the truth about you. You are Love.

But how can I know you are Love? How can I know you are beautiful? How can I know you are a blessing?

The Seed Inspiration to Awaken

If there is one thing that I have learned in my romance with the Divine, it is that I awaken through Divine inspiration. Inspiration appears, it activates my curiosity, and I glean a possibility where none seemed to exist before. I open to the possibility, ask for and surrender to the unknown blessings of the Divine, and more inspiration blesses my consciousness. Surprisingly and joyfully throughout my life, I have witnessed Divine Grace reveal Truth in clever and loving ways.

When I was six years old, I asked big questions about creation and God. Adults were unable to guide me and were mildly amused that a young child would ask such things. In their discomfort they brushed me off unceremoniously. I believed I was completely alone in life trying to answer these questions. So, I turned my attention to the Source and asked that I be guided by God directly.

What prompted a young child to want to know the secrets of the Universe and to seek direct mentorship from the Divine? When I think of myself at that time, the questions just came to me, dropping into my awareness. It was, most likely, Divine inspiration itself.

When I was eight years old, God came to me in a dream to play hide and seek in a bedroom. In the game, I searched in all the places where I thought that a person might hide: in the shadows under the bed, behind the door and in the dark closet. No luck.

God spoke clearly into the room instructing me, *"You will not find me in the darkness."*

I woke up a little wiser, moderately surprised, very curious, and extremely excited to play this game with God. I became a detective and followed the clues everywhere. I understood the most basic aspect of the instruction; I knew that I was to align my life with Light and Divine guidance to ultimately find God. I did not think there was much more to it. I was determined to find the Divine and I believed I could.

I was a serious but deeply curious child who preferred to be with adults rather than children. I never played with toys, but I took great delight in organizing adventure games with groups of children, solving puzzles and math equations, and figuring out dynamics among people. A spark, a seed of mystery was planted in my consciousness. God invited me into a mysterious game, and I fell for the romance, the puzzle and the promise-hope of an answer.

Unaware as a child, a deeply profound teaching was imbedded into the dream, which revealed itself more and more throughout my life as I grew in Wisdom. I believe that even deeper levels of the Wisdom will be revealed right to the end of my life. For now, I am pleasantly aware of the *game* that I have been playing to discover the Divine and the revelations that have blessed my awareness. I will reveal more about this later.

Although aligned with God and blessed with the awakening of consciousness, my childhood was less than idyllic. I grew up in a dysfunctional family. Both of my parents were emotionally unavailable, had addictions, and were periodically abusive to each other as well as with me and my sisters. I knew my parents were doing the best they could and that they loved us in their own way. Our basic physical needs were met, we were relatively safe, and they supported us in many practical ways.

I was also keenly aware of the irreconcilable inequities, inconsistencies, and imbalances in the dynamics between adults and children in families, education, entertainment, and religion. Like you, as a child I was at the whim of adults who were overwhelmed with their responsibilities and societal pressures, and who were emotionally damaged by their own upbringing. They taught and embodied societal and ancestral beliefs that had emotionally, energetically, physically, spiritually, and mentally enslaved and damaged successive generations until we arrived where we are today.

As I grew into my teens, I experienced deep depression. I was not only affected by my personal circumstances, but I was keenly and empathically aware of great suffering within those around me and throughout the world. This took its toll on my mind and my health.

As a teen, the massacre of thousands of people in Tiananmen Square in 1989 triggered one of my darkest times. My spirit was crushed. That darkness deepened when tens of thousands of Bosnian Muslim women experienced systematic, genocidal rape during the Bosnian War in the early 90's. When it all became too much to bear, I shut myself away in my bedroom and grieved continuously for weeks. I was on a precipice. My heart was breaking as I opened to the great suffering of these women and the world. The sadness was so great that I wanted to escape the suffering. For two weeks I laid on the floor wailing with deep grief. I felt an overwhelming urge to leave my body permanently and wanted to die.

At the darkest and most painful point, instead of me leaving my body, something powerful and monumental activated within me. It most likely came from my pleas and questions to God for those who were suffering. Ultimately, I cannot pinpoint what I said or what changed me. Somehow, in a moment, I was guided to love the world, as well as to stay open and aware of the suffering but not let it destroy me. Since then I have been blessed with a growing embodiment of unconditional love and with greater wisdom as to why the suffering of the world exists, as well as how to begin affecting change in the world.

These experiences of darkness and suffering served to wake me up to incredible compassion, spiritual abilities, and states of consciousness.

Deep Questions

In the beginning God created the heaven and the earth.
~Genesis 1:1

Genesis reveals to us that the Eternal Divine is the creator of the Universe as we know it.

I believe all of us have within us the seeds of curiosity about the mystery of creation and creator. We may ask what or who is God? Who am I? What is this existence all about? Why do people suffer?

Why would God allow me and others to suffer? How can I alleviate my suffering or the suffering of others?

Answers can be found in sacred texts, in nature, and within our own hearts.

The Creator of All both hides and reveals the story of Truth in creation. Within creation nature is a Divine teacher imbued with God's fingerprints and brushstrokes. Look to the seed that grows in the darkness of the soil. One day a dormant seed made of carbon, hydrogen, nitrogen, phosphorus, and oxygen is impregnated with the Divine spark. It carries a blueprint that inspires it. That seed feels called to something. It blindly follows the call and finds its way in the darkness, sometimes struggling and searching.

In its struggles and search, it is growing. It may not even know it is growing. It is just searching, course correcting, moving around obstacles, finding its way. Until one day that little seedling that has rooted in the earth, pops out into the light. It then surrenders to the light and bolts toward it, tracking and following it.

Each day when darkness falls the growing plant rests. There is an inner calling for the light to return; the young plant expects the light to return. And when the light dawns upon the earth that seedling surrenders. In the end, it is grown by both the light that it reaches toward and the dark earth that it is rooted within. The plant is still faced with challenges as it relies on circumstances outside of its control: rain, temperature, and predators. However, its connection and devotion to the light is sealed.

Look at the celebration of light in a flower or plant. See how they reach toward it, fully receptive, fully surrendered. The sun shines its light upon the whole planet regardless of whether a particular plant chooses to receive it or not. So too, God shines Divine Love-Sound-Light vibrations through all of creation, whether you choose to receive them or not.

So too are you nurtured. You are born into the darkness of this confused world of illusion. You carry the blueprint of Truth, a mysterious treasure map, hidden in the depths of your spiritual heart center.

Being in the darkness is challenging and devastating. I have felt lost in depths of darkness: fear, rejection, hopelessness, helplessness, depression, anxiety, and suicidal ideation. Most people have experienced some aspects of suffering. Rare are those who have lived a life of persistent joy from cradle to grave.

While it may not seem so, this world is a blessing for you to go from God Love into darkness and then to approach God Love again. I use *God Love* to refer to the field of Love from where we come and to which we return.

The mind tries try to solve the confusion of darkness and disconnection, but it does not know how. Resolving the darkness occurs with the Light of Divine Truth and Wisdom, which is the revelation of Love. Staying in the power of Love and listening to the call within the heart reveals Love, which you are.

Suffering

But why would this be? Why would we opt into a life where suffering exists for so many people? Why would God make us suffer like this? There are two answers that I will briefly touch upon.

Knowing Oneself

Not knowing who we are creates great suffering. When we believe we are the body or the mind, we fall for the dance of illusion or darkness. When we awaken to Truth, we learn that we are Divine Souls that are having an experience that is very unique. As a Soul, you enter into a body vehicle that grows within your mother. Then you and the body are birthed into the world. As the body grows, you learn how to operate it. But you are not the body.

Observe the way a baby learns first to train its hand to come to its mouth. Initially it sees the hand and learns that it can command the hand. Then it tries to bring it to itself. Babies are not initially precise in their movements. It takes many tries and a great deal of practice to master the muscles to be under their command. Until one day, just the thought of its hand coming to its mouth, makes it so. We learn every skill this way. We often believe we are the body because the body is extremely rapid, almost seamless, in doing what we expect of it.

Vedism, Judaism, Christianity, Sikhism, Islam, and many other religious traditions all refer to the One True God. Think about the field of the Divine: the one, the only. If there is only one True God, if none other exists but the Divine, then everything must be of God and must be one with God, even if we are blocked from knowing so. "For by him and through him and to him are all things."[2] If everything is created by God, through God and for God, you are significant to creation and are purposefully and Divinely created.

"… And to him" we return, just like each drop of water from around the world eventually returns to the ocean. When the water droplet falls from a cloud, or moves down a stream, it is not the ocean, but it is of the ocean. It may forget it is of the ocean, as it moves through each incarnation as snowflake, hail, raindrop, dew drop, perspiration, steam, running water, and still water. The return is imprinted within its blueprint by the ocean itself. And then one day the droplet returns and becomes one with the ocean again.

The Creation is in the Creator,
and the Creator is in the Creation,
totally pervading and permeating all places.
~ Sri Guru Granth Sahib 1349

Of course, this means little to you until you experience your Divine significance in its fullness. The moment for direct experiential oneness with the Divine is in perfect timing, so there is no rush. Resting into the knowing that everything is being revealed for you in its Divine timing may help free you from some of the fear and anxiety around your current situation and suffering. Allow yourself to be aware of your Divine beauty as a distant star that guides you on your path. And yet that star exists with you right here, right now. *"The kingdom of God is within you."*[3]

As you become re-acquainted with God's Love of you, this world looks and feels very different. You begin to feel a deep joyous peace

20

and equanimity. As you surrender to Divine mentorship the world, despite its conflicts, shines in a new way. Everyone and everything is more and more beautiful with each passing day. Sacred texts take on deeper meanings and reveal profound Truths hidden in plain sight. As you increasingly allow yourself to be aligned with the Divine, you receive creative energy and insight for actions that make real change.

Mystics from various traditions, like Rumi, Attar of Nishapur, Hildegard of Bingen, Saint Teresa of Ávila, St. John of the Cross, Nanak, Patanjali, Mansur al-Hallaj and Kabir demonstrate surrender to Divine mentorship beautifully and uniquely in their experiences with Divine Union that they attempted to share with the world. Along this path there are challenges, tests, responsibilities, and deep, sometimes uncomfortable, healing. I can attest to this. Even when you are challenged, exhausted, and confused, always remember to align yourself with the Divine to come home to the Truth of you.

A person might ask, "How is it that I don't know I am Divine?" If you were Divine and wanted to know yourself, how could you see yourself if you were the only thing that existed? Might you make yourself forget, so you could get to know yourself without the influence of omniscience? Might you do this from an incalculable number of stories, angles, and approaches? Is it possible that forgetting your Divinity could completely create such disorientation that you might make decisions that would throw you and others deeper into suffering?

Yet, what if there were fail-safes worked into the game of awakening, such as Divine Grace, mentors, God-devoted communities, spiritual practices that open and align us with Divine Truth and Wisdom, and Holy Beings to assist and guide us. Jesus is one such Divine mentor who instructs, *"I am the way, the truth, and the life. No one can come to the Father except through me."*[4] Jesus offers mentorship to those who are ready to align with Christ Consciousness, which is laid out by his teachings, like a map, to know God.

Christ Consciousness is Unconditional Love. Unconditional Love is automatic forgiveness. It means, *I love and accept you no matter what you have done*, which erases your debt, which means *there's nothing to be forgiven anymore, so just let your Divinity shine, oh beautiful being.* Jesus offers a brand-new covenant that never existed before. You can access it right now or you can move through the steps at any pace you choose. Either way… the path is revealed by Jesus the Christ.

The path is also revealed in other traditions such as Taoism, which is an ancient philosophy of living in the natural world. In the *Tao de Ching,* which literally means *the Book of the Way and its Power,* Lao Tzu offers the way to get back to being your Authentic Spiritual Self in oneness living in Divine Consciousness. The Tao teaches there is no separation in the Divine Oneness.[5]

To enter into our Divinity one of the steps we need to overcome is our attachment to the web of lies the world believes about who we are and why we are here that keeps us on the rollercoaster of suffering. It requires we abandon all lies and illusion for Divine Truth. The way to renew ourselves in the Truth of our Divinity is by aligning with Divine mentorship. Revelation 21:7 declares, *"He who overcomes shall inherit all things, and I will be his God and he shall be My son."*

An ancient Sanskrit Vedic text shares, "As long as we think we are the ego, we feel attached and fall into sorrow. But realize that you are the Self, the Lord of life, and you will be freed from sorrow. When you realize that you are the Self, supreme source of light, supreme source of love, you transcend the duality of life and enter into the unitive state."[6]

Some people think it is egotistical and sacrilegious to believe we could be Divinity. During Jesus' time, a great number of people believed that his declaration of Divinity was blasphemous, and he died on the cross at the hands of those people. Yet he was free of the influence of their beliefs. Their limiting beliefs did not stop his ministry, nor did they stop his Ascension into Christhood.

So, let me mentor you right here and right now. When you have a belief that accessing Divinity is not possible for any living person, when you think you are not worthy or your neighbor is not worthy, the negative thought comes because of the ego's allegiance to ancestral programming from ideas or memes, which have created so much suffering over millennia.

Allow yourself to be free of any negative ideas about yourself and others. If you have made mistakes, then with all your heart ask for forgiveness from God. If you ask, you truly need to accept forgiveness to make it stick, which means you forgive yourself too. When you accept forgiveness for yourself, you rise up in your awareness that you, just like everyone else, is worthy of forgiveness. Since God offers forgiveness to you and everyone, be like God and forgive your parents, teachers, politicians, neighbors, friends, frenemies, arch nemeses… and everyone.

Think of the significance of this: The Divine could be doing anything and yet God is here with you, is here to serve you. The Divine is at your service at every moment to return you to the Grace of your Divinity.

When you approach Divinity, you become like the Divine in that your heart is oriented toward unconditionally serving humanity. You end up aligned with the Will of God, which in this case is about bringing everyone home to God in the fullness of our Divinity. Christ, Buddhas, Bodhisattvas, Divine Saints, and Holy Masters all serve humanity. That is their *modus operandi*.

Touching into the Grace of the Divine is a humbling experience that sets the ego-mind at ease, fills the heart with compassion and unconditional Love, and allows the reception of Divine Truth and Wisdom so you may truly serve your community.

In Buddhism, we learn that the Buddha uses *expedient means* to assist people in reaching enlightenment: their True state. God knows precisely how to call you, how to awaken you to the power and glory of your re-union with the Divine.

Although you may not yet have experienced your Divinity, the Divine guides you to your Divinity. Each one of us has a unique path to the return to the Divine. Listen to the call that shines out from everything. If you are ready surrender to the guidance of the Divine, use the gifts you have been blessed with and share them lovingly with the world to uplift others.

Free Will

The second answer to why suffering exists is free will. Free will is a gift from God to allow us to choose for ourselves. At any given moment we are free to respond to life however we choose. This also includes whether or not we choose to explore a relationship with the Divine. God allows everything that exists, or it simply would not exist. It is not God that makes us suffer. Our individual and collective choices contribute to whether we suffer or not, as there are consequences to all our choices.

When we attack others, lie, cheat, steal, judge, ignore, fear, or compartmentalize, we create our own personal suffering and we contribute to the suffering of others involved.

When we allow women to be marginalized or physically harmed, when we allow humans to be enslaved economically or in dangerous work, or when we allow our environment to be destroyed, we create our own suffering.

Someone might ask, "What about the death of a child? What has that child ever done to deserve to die?" As tragic as one might think it is for a child to die of natural causes or an accident, we are supposing that death is worse than life. We do this because those who survive are deeply traumatized by the death and physical loss of a loved one, especially a baby or child.

Death is not a punishment for doing something wrong. It is a holy sacrament into the mystery of what many call heaven, which I believe is the field of *God Love*.

We also do not know the will of that soul, including what they chose to experience in this life and the duration of the life they chose to live. No one can predict the timing of anyone's death and all durations of life are represented in this existence.

No matter how dark and wayward our creation, God allows us to create with free will regardless of the immediate outcome. When we see the consequences, we have the opportunity to make amends and to learn to do things differently. Some people learn quickly; some people cycle through suffering many times before they learn. Yet all is allowed.

Like a loving parent who watches their child learning to walk, the Divine is the ultimate parent letting us experiment, fall down, hurt ourselves, cry, get back up, and try again. God allows us to learn even when it may hurt, yet we are never abandoned. When a child falls down and gets back up multiple times, and finally learns to walk, look at how solid they become. Their mastery over their legs and stomach muscles, and their ability to balance becomes intrinsic and their new natural skill state.

How many people know that Maya Angelou worked as a prostitute and a madam when she was a struggling mother long before she became an internationally celebrated poet, writer, and civil rights activist? Spiritual innovator, author, and speaker Byron Katie first suffered from depression and an addiction to codeine and alcohol before she woke up from her suffering.

Spiritual teacher Gangaji suffered in disillusionment and longing until her unexpected awakening in 1990. Internationally influential spiritual teacher and author of *The Power of Now* Eckhart Tolle endured depression until he experienced an "inner transformation" in his late 20's.

When you suffer deeply, you hope there is more to life than suffering and you crave relief. When you feel alone, you long for connection to others. Ultimately connection is the Truth of you, as that which is connected to all. Many people suffer because the teachings and beliefs that have passed on from generation to generation are lies about ourselves that have resulted in disconnection from our true nature. Collectively, we know something is not quite right with how we have been doing things.

The Divine loves you, knows your suffering, and is with you as you struggle out of the darkness. The Love that the Divine has for you is indescribable. Just touching into God's Love for you overwhelms my heart and brings me to my knees. Oh, how the Divine loves you. If only you knew. Let me share my experience of how God revealed deep, abiding, unconditional Love for us:

You are the creation of God. You are the beauty of God. There is not one wrinkle, hair, nail, or cell that was not created by the Divine. God is the master architect, sculptor, and admirer of you and of creation Itself. If you look at a wrinkle on your face, that is the Love of God written upon you. The curves, the contours, the space surrounding you, the masterful etching is the deep story of you. Here, there, and everywhere, God knows you, knows Creation.

Everything that exists is the surrender of God to you. Everything that exists is the Divine loving Creation. God is unconditional love. God allows everything, witnesses it and still loves us. Even when you think you are lost, broken, or alone, God is there with you, loving you, beckoning you to return to Love. However, God does not force you to love God. The Divine patiently, beautifully, and humbly asks at your feet, "May I love you?"

Chapter 2 - Seed

Those mountains that you have been carrying,
you were only supposed to climb.
~ Najwa Zebian

You were born the most magnificent, powerful embodiment of love and creation. You came from Love, a field of loving connection. And those who were emotionally available felt joy looking at you, holding you, caring for you, smelling you, watching you explore your surroundings, and were deeply affected by the beauty of you.

Even if you had a rough start to life, even if you had parents who were emotionally unavailable, just like every other baby who has ever come into this life you affected people so deeply as the embodiment of love. At some point someone was affected by your beauty even if they got distracted later by the suffering of life.

You were born as pure wisdom of loving connection. Remember when you were very young, if others were mean to you or neglectful of your needs you knew that something was wrong or off and that it should be another way, a loving way.

If you now feel disconnected from yourself, others, or life, and if you feel unsure of yourself, depressed, alone, anxious, or fearful, then ask yourself what happened to that powerful, wise, loving, connected version of you?

You may have your theories, remembrances of betrayal, or painful experiences where life *seemed* to tell you something negative about yourself. Periodically, experiences occurred convincing you to believe negative and absolutely hurtful ideas about you.

Slowly you exchanged the Truth of you for a variety of lies, such as "I'm not good enough," "I'm not important enough," or "I'm not worthy of love."

No one consciously tried to convince you of these lies. People, unconscious of their behaviors, acted in ways that were in contrast and in conflict with the Truth of love and connection. Because you expected love and connection their actions confused your mind.

The mind abhors confusion. It feels powerless and vulnerable when there are conflicting beliefs. To feel settled, the mind has to resolve confusion. The mind will do anything to resolve confusion including making you wrong, blaming you, or rejecting you. However, the mind is crafty; it does it in a way that is not too painful. The mind hides the lie and creates a rationalization without you being aware. If it was too painful, you would want to die. Over time the mind can become dangerously littered with lies, leaving some people at the edge of not wanting to live with the pain.

Every lie about yourself creates disconnection. The mind helps out by creating distractions, which can become addictive, because they provide temporary relief from the suffering. However, at some point distractions become boring and dull and we are forced to feel the suffering the mind has created.

At the same time, the lies we hold within us are an energy that causes interference in our physical and energetic body. The stress of these lies affects the immune system, nervous system, and the flow of energy throughout the body. Interestingly, certain lies or emotional conflicts result in specific symptoms or diseases. Many people do not address the lies of the mind until they reach a physical rock bottom.

The mind also lies to you about other people and the world. It tries to convince you that others will reject you or hurt you. It tries to make you safe by determining who is 'good' or 'bad,' 'safe' or 'dangerous.'

Sometimes we participate indirectly or directly with other people in collective lies about groups of people to help us to feel safer. Sometimes we distance ourselves from others who have different beliefs to keep us comfortable. Yet strangely, when our mind becomes polarized, we construct walls. We then feel worse and more fearful of our safety being compromised. When fears and judgements about others arise in your mind, the only true way out is to shine your awareness on the lies that you have unconsciously allowed and cultivated.

At some point, in the beginning of your life, you accepted your first false belief about you. In accepting the belief, you began to program yourself as that belief and you anticipated the reality of that belief. Fearful anticipation of something happening again, or confirmation of something you do not want to be, attracts the very circumstances you fear, and then your mind affirms the belief.

I have observed the underlying lies in clients who work with me. These lies are rooted in what the mind convinced them of when they were children. Common lies that children tell themselves include: I'm not enough, I'm not worthy of love, there's something wrong with me, I can't trust myself, I'm not safe, I'm a burden, it's not safe to need anything, I can't do anything right, I have to keep my mom/dad happy, I'm ugly, or I'm rejectable. Also common, many children believe that to be acceptable by others they have to determine right from wrong, good from bad, and live by what is dictated as 'right' and 'good.'

If it is unattainable to be 'right' and/or 'good,' because outside rules are too stringent or a child has been labelled as a 'bad' boy or girl, a person might need to reject the rule maker and become the rebel to feel safe and in control.

The most common root causes of these beliefs are the child's awareness that there is a lack of true connection between them and their parent. What children need most in stressful situations, especially when they are crying for any reason (including what we might call a 'temper tantrum), is a hug and being told, "You matter to me, I love you so much. I'm here for you. Let's figure this out together."

If ever a child makes a mistake, no matter how big, they need to hear in words and loving actions, "Even though you made a mistake you are loved. There are consequences to your actions, and I'm here for you. I know you are just learning how to be in life. Let me help you navigate through life." Kids are scared, uncertain and just finding their way. Be a loving mentor. Extend your wisdom patiently.

The truth is, we all need unconditional love and support from others and ourselves when we make unwise choices and mistakes. To be shunned, discarded, abandoned, or labelled 'bad' is painful at any age. To continue to believe that we are bad, or others are bad, as a result of that unhealthy behavior of our parents, is unnecessary and creates suffering.

Some parents are emotionally disabled and just cannot offer a child what they need emotionally. If a parent is consistently emotionally unavailable when the child invites them to share what they are learning or to spend time playing, the child can feel deeply unworthy of love and attention.

If you took on any lies about yourself when you were young, I wish a parent or a mentor had explained to you that other people's behavior had nothing to do with you. I wish someone had shared with you that many people in the world are feeling sad, lonely, frustrated, fearful, angry, and hurt. If someone had explained that hurt people behave in hurtful ways, then you might have remained strong in knowing you were lovable, acceptable, and powerful. I invite you to choose these healthy beliefs today!

The truth is, if your parents did not accept you as you were, guide you lovingly, or make time to meet your emotional needs, it is because of:

- Their level of consciousness;
- Their overwhelming circumstances at the time;
- The general programming they received from their parents and society about who they are;

- Specific programming from their ancestors, parents, and society about how to raise children; and
- The lies they believe about themselves about being not lovable, not acceptable, or not enough.

You have been the recipient of generations of programming of a variety of lies. Spanning back 20 generations in your lineage, each parent's parent totals over a million immediate ancestors for you alone. In approximately 500 years, you have a multitude of beliefs, energies, and DNA combining and influencing your existence from all these people in your lineage.

Your parents' behavior has nothing to do with whether you are lovable or not. If another child, instead of you, had been born to your parents, they would have treated them in the same way. It has everything to do with your mom and dad's programming from what they learned from their parents and other adults. They did not know this, not fully. They have been unaware. They did not have the same opportunity to awaken that you have. If they had been fully conscious, they would have taken steps to heal.

You have the opportunity right here, right now to wake up to the truth about you; you are lovable because you are the embodiment of Love. Even if you have unconsciously accepted the subtle and not-so subtle programming of your ancestors, you can now choose to let the light that is you shine. You can choose to let go of the need for your parents or family to be conscious or to know how to meet your needs. They could not and may never be able to meet some of your needs due to their own limitations.

Be grateful that you were born with a greater knowing of truth and illumination. If you had been born as your parents, you would have made the same choices that they did and had been as stuck as they were. Forgive them for being born into a time of relative darkness without the resources and consciousness that you have today. Forgive them for they did not know how to do anything other than what they were shown. They were, and perhaps still are, stuck in the illusion of lies about themselves and the world.

See your birth into this life as a turning point from the darkness: the beginning of the return to the light. You were born with enough love and connection to know that something else was possible in this world, and it is still possible. Let Love shine out from you! Be the remembrance of Love. Reactivate Truth. Cultivate loving connection with the Divine, friends, yourself, your family and the world.

It is such a marvelous time in existence! Simply, you are the one your ancestors have been waiting for to heal the dysfunction of your family. You are the one I have been waiting for because when you heal, you make healing possible for others in the world. Your longing for love and connection is an indication that you are bringing in the light of consciousness to bring about beautiful change in the world. Let yourself remember and connect with who you are. Let the Love that you are shine into the world for all to experience.

Why is it so joyful to shine Love into my life?

Chapter 3 - Divine Mentorship

Forget the past.
The vanished lives of all men are dark with many shames.
Human conduct is ever unreliable until anchored in the Divine.
Everything will improve if you are making a spiritual effort now.
~ Sri Yukteswar

Intentional Prayer

Today's journey loosely began when I sat to meditate for the day with a group of people. My intention was to surrender deeper to the Divine. As I settled in my seat, I briefly recalled two photographic self-portraits that I had taken one afternoon in 2004.

In the first self-portrait I chose to pose as Green Tara. In Buddhism, Tara is known as a Buddha or Bodhisattva of compassion. There are multiple forms of Tara in various colors. Green Tara is known as the Buddha of enlightenment. Her name means "star" or "to cross over the ocean." As I sat for the photo, I imitated Green Tara's body pose and mudra (gesture) with one hand as I held a lotus flower in the other hand.

In the second portrait, I surrendered to the Divine on my knees with a big full moon in the background. In the photo I was on my knees, sitting on my heels, with my arms outstretched to the sky. I evoked a moment of surrender to the Divine, from when I almost died from intense heat stroke in 1999, under the full moon. You can feel surrender when you look at the photo. The 'surrendered portrait' was the most powerful of the two photos.

I dismissed these images from my mind as I thought they were a distraction from my meditation. In that moment I was unaware of their significance. However, this memory became divinely woven into my experience by the end of today and was incredibly symbolic and prophetic.

I usually choose an intention each time I sit to meditate. Today, I sat with my eyes closed and entered into a focused intention on Divine Surrender. Internally I began repeating over and over again:

I choose Divine Grace, I choose God, I choose Christ, I choose the Holy Spirit, I choose the Divine Mother, I choose Divine Truth, I choose Divine Love, I choose Divine Wisdom.

Simultaneously, I envisioned my heart full of all that I chose to embody. Within a very short amount of time, I felt both my energetic crown center and heart center open. This feeling state is interesting, it feels like vibrational openness, best described as the opposite of pressure. An opened crown chakra gives us access to higher states of consciousness and Divine Wisdom and Truth. When the heart center blossoms, we feel deeply connected, compassionate, loving, and peaceful. Curiously, the Flower of Heaven appeared as a type of energy-image-idea in my awareness. I had never heard about the Flower of Heaven, so I was deeply intrigued.

The Divine is a great storyteller weaving Wisdom and Truth in cheeky and clever ways. The mysterious gift of the Flower of Heaven was a taste to capture my attention and evoke the invitation of God within me. Given that the Flower was from Heaven, I decided to say *YES!* to this unknown flower. To open further, I prayed:

Teach me dear, Highest God. I surrender to Divine Truth. I choose the embodiment of Divine Love, Wisdom and Truth. I choose the Flower of Heaven within me. Whatever I experience, let it be for all humanity, for all people. Guide and teach me to surrender to you.

The seed of the Flower of Heaven was now planted in my heart center.

Inspirational Invitation

The Divine is a masterful teacher who knows just how to reveal divinity. The most glorious way to teach children or adults of all ages is through inspirational invitation and mentorship. For deep learning, inspiring others to learn from you is a blessing. The difference between a child who is taught piano from force, even with 'good' intentions, is in stark contrast to a child who feels deeply inspired to learn music.

Spirituality falls into the same guidelines. Any religious or spiritual path to God or learning of any kind that involves indoctrination, shame, rejection, force, or have-to's will result in depression, anxiety, rebellion, resistance, illusion, and suffering.

If you choose to be a teacher of any kind, first free the other fully from your expectation, which means allowing them to choose their own path and to explore it in their own way. Choose to become creative, flexible, and a great listener and observer of their needs while teaching. You bring your expertise and foundational framework, but be fluid in your expression. Be curiously mindful of the audience: the student.

Let all mentorship be loving and kind. At times, you may need to educate or inform another person at home, work, in a relationship, or in school because they are being hurtful, are not stepping up, or are not taking responsibility. Chastising, shaming, or dismissing them will only shut them down from learning or meeting you where you would like them to be.

Rather than disciplining someone who makes a mistake with frustration or expectation, instead be the invitation. Teach them lovingly how to be intrinsically disciplined by inspiring mastery with your actions, educating about the possibilities of advancement when disciplined, freeing them to make mistakes and to try again with openness, and inviting them to have fun in the process.

My five-year-old son declared he will be a ninja when he grows up. One day while sitting at his piano he was resistant to practicing. Nothing I said inspired him. I felt frustrated, not by his resistance, but by my 'failure' to convince him to do his music homework. Inspiration hit me and I shared with him, "You know, there are ninja piano players in the world!" He was intrigued, so I showed him an online video of the fastest piano player in the world. He became inspired and embraced his lessons.

When we are moved by intrinsic discipline, we can access deeper insight, skill, advancement, and mastery in an area of study or work. When someone makes a mistake or does not know how to do something, guide them lovingly. When you are encouraging someone to up level their game, always uplift them in the process. Think of training, educating, or mentoring like taking a blindfolded person by the hand to guide them in unchartered territory. When others make mistakes, trust it is because they do not know any better or see the bigger picture.

If you are a student, free yourself to learn what moves, nourishes, and intrigues you. Empty yourself to learn from the experience and skill of a teacher. If you are resistant to learning anything, check to see if you are being triggered by an unconscious false belief about yourself or about learning. Some of my clients have come with false beliefs that they were stupid, stuck, or blocked. Others have come with a protective resistance to any teacher. Identifying the lies opens you to intrinsic motivation and deeper learning. The keys to learning include readiness, willingness, discipline, receptivity, creativity, and celebration.

People can learn anything, including music, and still feel empty inside. They might know the most facts, they may memorize and be able to do advanced math, they may be technically skilled beyond any other person, but magic, aliveness, and intrinsic beauty is missing. When a person is freed to experiment, explore, and be inspired to learn, they are captivated by intrinsic motivation. They surrender to the beauty of music, math, geography, chemistry, physics, literature, art, philosophy, or law. In surrender to beauty, the unthinkable and transcendent happens; their experience becomes indescribable.

We recognize these artists as masters of their field. As they allow creation to unfold from within them, they become vessels surrendered to the process and the dance of creation. Creation weaves its way in, around and through them. We appreciate these artists because they touch us deeply and connect us to the beauty of creation and the expression of what we call art or artistry, whether it be Albert Einstein, Picasso, John Lennon, Vandana Shiva, Greta Thunberg, or Steve Jobs.

When we are moved, truly moved by a performance, painting, story, technology, or an inspirational person, we touch into the revelation of ourselves and the beauty within. We also touch into the beauty of the Divine. When we look with unconditional love, even that which we might have called ugly, dark, unfamiliar, uncomfortable, or rejectable becomes beautiful, too.

Jean Vanier, the founder of L'Arche, an international federation of communities for people with developmental disabilities and those who assist them, attested to the power of people with disabilities to open the hearts and awaken the humanity and self-acceptance of intellectually abled persons by giving them the opportunity to learn to love by accepting people as they are. Jean created places where people could interact with people with intellectual disabilities in ways where they were equals, where the intellectually abled could experience unconditional acceptance from the disabled. In the face of not knowing how to be in the world of the disabled, he personally experienced and observed that those who are considered the most incapable and weakest enable those who consider themselves more capable or strong, to recognize and relax into their own vulnerability.

Mr. Vanier received the 2015 Templeton Prize, which identifies and honors entrepreneurs of the spirit for their exceptional contribution to affirming life's spiritual dimension. In his acceptance speech, Jean shared,

> "Universal peace can only come if we develop and awaken those very human qualities, hidden under the more superficial needs for power and of winning, which lead us to welcome reality. These qualities are those linked to the heart – the capacity to love people, to respect them deeply, to live authentic relationships with others, to yearn for truth and justice in the huge family of humanity; qualities of humility, of forgiveness and of compassion for those who are weaker and in need; in short to seek the wisdom of the heart."[7]

Humanitarian Mother Teresa held the hands of lepers, the crippled, and the blind. She took basic care of the most rejected and gave the poorest of the poor in Calcutta a clean, loving place to live and die in dignity. She saw beauty in every human being. Her work extended across the globe as she established homes for the orphaned, sick and dying.

Love activists like Vanier and Mother Teresa inspire us to move beyond our fears, to see all humans as worthy of dignity, acceptance, and love. Think of it this way, if we love and accept everyone as they are, we educate our own minds to love and accept ourselves just as we are, without needing to be successful, wealthy, or useful.

The mind applies all rules you make toward others or allow from others, to you. If we reject a person with an intellectual disability, then we judge ourselves when our mental capabilities decline. When we judge an elderly person for not being able to move fast enough or be interesting enough to spend time with, we preemptively shame ourselves for our elder experience. Loving or accepting others unconditionally allows us to love and accept ourselves.

Divine Mentorship

Today is a day of loving awakening. I invite you into Love.

The Divine invited me into Love. God revealed the surrender by being The Surrender and majestic teachings were revealed. Expressing this experience in words is tricky, because it is not an idea of the mind. It is a deep, embodied, experiential knowing in the eternal ever-changing nowness of creation. I will do the best I can to share this experience.

Unexpectedly the Divine surrendered to me by merging into me to teach me surrender. It was as if God was kneeling before every aspect of me and kneeling inside of me at the same time saying, "I lovingly serve you." I was deeply moved and humbled to receive this gift. All of me is loved and accepted. All of me is loving and accepting.

In surrendering in and to me, there was no 'me,' just God. 'I' surrendered all, especially the small ego 'me' to the glory of Divine Love, which itself is Surrender.

Then, step by step, God reminded me and demonstrated to me how to surrender to the beauty of you and to love you just as you are, no matter what you have done and no matter what lies you have believed about yourself. Through Divine Love of you, God declared to me the beauty of you! You, dear beautiful creation of God, are glorious! You are celebrated by the Divine!

God revealed in me the glory of loving you, the glory of serving you and the glory of surrendering to you. **When we serve, care for, and love each other we touch into God, we invite Love in, and we are transformed and blessed.** Surrender = Service = Love.

I asked to touch into as much of God's Love for us that I could take. The beauty was glorious, but near unbearable. If I experienced even an iota more of God's Love, I perceived I would be annihilated by the depth, breadth, fullness, and *everywhereness* of it. God revealed that Divine Love and Presence is constant and ever-present with all of us.

Ancient Chinese philosopher, writer, and teacher Lao-Tzu describes the service of the Divine when he shares:

> "The great Tao is vast. He is on the left and He is on the right. All creatures depend upon Him, and the care of them tires Him not. He brings creation to completion, without seeking reward. He provides for all His creation, but requires nothing for Himself, so He may be considered

small. All creatures turn to Him for their needs, yet He keeps nothing for Himself, thus He may be named 'the Supreme.' He does not consider Himself great and because of this He is truly Great."[8]

Each person, whether they are joyful or are suffering due to disharmony of the body, mind, or soul, deserves the love of the Divine. Every single person, no matter what, is loved by God.

Love each other as the Creator of Everything loves: unconditionally.

If you know people who are suffering, love them. Truly be of service. Even something as simple as a smile is loving and may be the only love or kindness gifted to them that day. Hug them, see them, love them, accept them unconditionally. Imagine they are lost children of the Divine, they are the Divine, and you are the gift connecting them to Love. At the same time that you love and accept them just as they are, you restore their Divinity and yours too.

Service is not about 'I'll do this, so I get that.' Simply, it is about seeing the suffering in the world and choosing to love the world. It is about letting individuals, collectives, or nations know: you matter, you are loved, and I accept you.

Service is also not about being better or more enlightened than another. It is about loving another as your equal. Unconditional love never expects the other to be different than they are. Nor does it place a person below another. If anything, unconditional love places the other above. However, this is only in relation to the ego mind and never at the expense of your own needs for safety, integrity, self-love and sovereignty.

If you do not know how to love or serve, then ask the Divine to teach you. If you are blocked from knowing love, choose and ask for all blockages to True Love to be transformed by the Grace of God. Love is the path to access your birthright, to know yourself as the blessing that you are, and to return you home to the Divine.

Inspiration through loving demonstration is the best way to teach anything. Truthfully, every action or non-action we choose in life teaches others and affects the overall field of creation.

When a nation allows their rainforest to be cut down, destruction and disharmony are taught. When a leader is bent on building a wall, physical or otherwise, disconnection is taught. When a CEO allows workers to be exploited, abuse is taught. When a teacher is hard on a student, shame is learned. When a parent leaves their baby to cry on its own, aloneness and separation is imparted. When the elderly are warehoused or forgotten, neglect becomes familiar in society.

Think about this last example. If we were to allow our grandparents or parents to live in questionable circumstances, where they are over medicated, malnourished and alone, what do you think your quality of life will be when you are an elder? What we do to others, we accept and we invite for ourselves.

Poetically, what we do for others we also do for the Divine. Jesus instructs, "*Truly I tell you, whatever you did for one of the least of these brothers and sisters of mine, you did for me.*"[9] Not only is the Divine stating the importance of those that many people might consider unworthy, but Jesus is alluding to the Oneness of the downtrodden and disenfranchised of society with himself.

In all things, you are invited to be a demonstration of peace and love toward yourself, your family, your neighbors, nature and the world.

The Blessing of Friendship with Children

When we love and protect each other and creation, **we ascend** into the presence of the Divine. When we lovingly connect with each other, **we ascend**. When we respect each other, **we ascend**.

Jesus, the Christ, is a beautiful teacher revealing the gift of loving each other. He shared Divine revelation, a new testament, a higher teaching. Christ came as the embodiment of Love, to teach us to love and serve each other and children. He shares, *"Whoever wants to be first must place himself last of all and be the servant of all."* Then *he took a child and had him stand in front of them. He put his arms around him and said to them, "Whoever welcomes in my name one of these children, welcomes me; and whoever welcomes me, welcomes not only me but also the one who sent me."*[10]

Jesus then shared, *"If anyone should cause one of these little ones to lose his faith in me, it would be better for that person to have a large millstone tied around his neck and be thrown into the sea."*[11] Causing a child to lose faith in Christ means losing faith in Christ consciousness, the I AM Presence. When we are in touch with Christ, we are in touch with our own Divinity. When a child learns separation and disconnection, they become disconnected from the Love that they are and are cast into illusion and suffering.

Jesus made something very clear. *"Let the children come to me. Don't stop them! For the Kingdom of Heaven belongs to those who are like these children. I assure you that whoever does not receive the Kingdom of God like a child will never enter it."*[12]

Children are closest to God. They reveal creation. They are the embodiment of Love and Connection. How do you feel when you hold a newborn? You can see Love emanating from a baby when they make googly eyes with you or when they look deep into your eyes. You can feel Love when your child reaches for your hand. You can hear Love when a child laughs or experience Love when they openly invite you to share what they are discovering.

The Divine beckons you through children. Children are the great inviters into play and joy. Listen and watch for their invitation. They are also witnesses to the revelation of creation and invite whomever is there to participate and to share in the glory of joy and creation. If you find it challenging, uncomfortable, or repulsive to be around children, it might be that as a child you felt unworthy of spending time with an adult, or you learned that children were to not be seen or heard among adults, or someone made you believe that as a child you were unacceptable. Be curious about your resistance as a gateway to healing it.

How you are with children has a lot to do with how you were directly mentored by the adults in your life when you were a child. For example, if a father is uncomfortable connecting with his baby, but is able to connect when his son becomes old enough to throw a football, that child may grow up having a similar pattern of the timing of connecting with their child. Most likely that father experienced the same pattern from his father.

You do not need to have a child to benefit from the Divine beauty of children. Spending quality time with children of friends or family is a great way to access the gift that children offer.

As a single parent, I know life can be challenging and can pull your attention in many directions. *Maya* or the illusions of this world encourage separation and disconnection between you and a child. Children need your attention above all else. The quality of your attention is the single most important gift you can give a child. The practice and path of connecting with a child is a gift to you, the child and the world. You choose what you create and what you focus your attention on in this life.

Connecting with a child is an incredible opportunity and gift for both you and the child. See through their eyes and invite them to teach you. They will feel delighted and inspired to assist you. Children are closer to God than you know. They are born as the embodiment of radiant Divine Love. When you hold a baby, it is so apparent. They evoke tenderness, love, and openness. That is God loving you through that baby! Such a blessing!

We are born into this life with a blankish slate. We are graced with the knowing of love and connection. We also come with both personal karma and ancestral baggage.

Soon after a baby is born, illusion comes in and begins teaching them lies, such as "you are not important," "you are not enough," "you are not worthy," or "there's no time for you." Guess who teaches children these lies? Mostly their parents transmit deep unconscious lies that they learned from their parents, school, and society. Then as a child moves into the world media, teachers, friends, and experiences begin to influence them.

I share this with you lovingly. Your most important job as a parent, or as a friend to a child, is to mentor children in a field of unconditional love and acceptance. Your gift is to see the rightness in them and reflect it back. You are the witness of the Divine in them.

Almost every child is born expecting love and connection to be available. They lose themselves each and every time we tell them or show them that neither is available. This can happen in the form of a harsh word, yelling at them, not making time for them, or sending them away for a time out.

It is wonderful to be physically present in the same space as a child. More importantly, a child needs you to be energetically present with them, to play with them, to listen to them and to show them you care.

Look them in the eyes and say, "You are so important to me." Then with your actions demonstrate your reverence for them by spending time interacting with them and mentoring them. Even if they do something 'wrong' be gentle. They are just learning how to *be* in this world. Truly they do not know much about the world. Assume when they make a mistake that they are encountering something new that they need to learn from. They need you to be their loving guide. Be of service to them. Keep the love that they are intact. Be a mirror of love.

If they 'act out,' it is always a call for love. If they make a 'mistake,' it is always a call for love. Teach them how to make better choices by mentoring them lovingly. If you find yourself reacting or experiencing anger or frustration with a child, then use it as a gateway to shine light and love upon the lies you were taught by your parents and ultimately by your ancestors. Take responsibility and make amends with that child by apologizing as soon as possible. Explain that your anger was not their fault, that **every person is responsible for their own emotions,** and that your anger was your responsibility. If you get angry with yourself when you make mistakes with children or anyone, then ask yourself, "Why did I react like that? What made me feel that way? What is the lie that I am believing about myself or them?" See Chapter 9 for the *Clarity Process* to assist you in identifying and clearing false beliefs.

Let your interactions with children be intentionally and purposefully loving, fun, and accepting. You can either strengthen a child in love and connection or you can plant seeds of self-doubt, self-rejection, and disconnection. The choice is yours.

Respect the Wisdom of Children

We are witnessing a time where children are rising up in their power as voices for inspirational change. They are mentoring their parents and older generations to actively begin to make major changes in evidence of glaring environmental and social issues that previous generations have taken too long to address. They feel the urgency for change because they know the long-term consequences that affect their future. Be curious and listen to their passionate messages and educated calls-to-action. Let yourself be inspired to contribute to change as best you can.

Chapter 4
Divine Love Song of Surrender

I am the light that is over all things.
I am all: from me all came forth, and to me all attained.
Split a piece of wood; I am there.
Lift up the stone, and you will find me there.
~ Gospel of Thomas, 77

Returning to the teachings God weaved for me during my meditation today, God inspired me to ask for a teaching about song. I asked the Creator to sing through me, and I surrendered to the revelation of song in many forms.

God sings through the artist. God sings through nature. God sings through me and you. God's song rings out in the ever-changing Nowness through every blade of grass, every rock face, every pattern, every gem, every sound, every mathematical equation, every bird, every petal, every smile, every tear, every space, and every atom.

I looked at some of the other people meditating and observed beautiful people with all range of shape, size and hair color. The Divine zoomed onto the creases in the fabric of their clothes and the strands of their hair saying, "*I AM there and there.*" Everywhere

I looked, the ceiling, the floor, every sound, every shape… *"I AM"* singing out. As we bear witness to the immense beauty of others the Divine is revealed and we are revealed to ourselves.

The Universe is sound vibration energy. The sound of the Divine, or the song of God, is recognized in Christianity as the Word of God and described in ancient Vedic texts as Om or Aum. It is believed that the sound OM is a primordial sound vibration from which all the manifest Universe emanates. From Ultimate Reality, from the Divine, creation is made manifest. Om is the manifest and the unmanifest Divine, the creation and the Creator and the Preserver and the Destroyer.

The very foundations of our Universe, of matter and thought, seem to be grounded in sound vibration. Everything in the Universe is made up of atoms that are constantly vibrating in a multitude of frequencies.[13]

Futurist and brilliant inventor, Nikola Tesla revealed, "If you want to find the secrets of the Universe, think in terms of energy, frequency and vibration." We know that each basic element of the known Universe vibrates at a different frequency. Temperature is a measure of molecular movement. Atoms and molecules vibrate faster when they heat up and slower when then cool down. Light energy also moves at different frequencies. Each color has its own frequency vibration.

Everything looks and sounds the way it does due to vibration. The range of human hearing extends from 20 to 20,000 Hertz. We cannot perceive below or above that range without technology. We believe the human eye registers sight, but sight really is the visual reception of sound vibration, too.

Look at the fabric on your couch or clothing; it is visual sound vibration. Some patterns on rugs or textiles are quite noisy, others are quiet. Now consider the flat, smooth, quiet surface of a glass table. How do each of them compare to the vibration of a leaf?

What about touch? With your hand feel some rough or smooth surfaces. As you do, you are feeling sound vibration. To tickle your mind, what is happening when you close your eyes and think about a color, shape, or object? Think of the whole scene of a sunset as a song with a range of vibrations. Or contemplate the vibration of the ocean with a multitude of color, texture, and form vibrations.

> *The heavens declare the glory of God;*
> *the skies proclaim the work of his hands.*
> *Day after day they pour forth speech;*
> *night after night they reveal knowledge.*
> *~ Psalm 19:1-2*

The song vibration of God is the surrender of God to you. Here, there, and everywhere, throughout creation, the Divine surrenders to you, sings to you, through you, in and around you.

All the while God loves you, and is available to surrender to you at any given moment even if you are not yet aware or you believe you are lost. The Divine loves you, even if you choose to turn your back to loving you, even if you choose to turn your back to the Divine.

You are song. Your very existence is song. Your name is song. Your every movement is song. How you speak to people and what you think about them or yourself is song. What song do you choose to sing?

The Divine knows the song you sing. Every note, tone, silent pause, and nuance is known, loved and witnessed by God. You are known.

The Love of the Creator is many things and it is one thing. It is God's Love of you, your Love of God, and your Love of others and creation. Ultimately, it is the Divine loving the Divine. Let yourself *be* the Love of God to create the life you choose.

But how can I *be* the Love of God?

Co-creating an amazing loving world, begins by letting go of the need to change others or the world because we perceive it to be flawed. Love the world as it is. Make change by determining what it is that you choose to experience.

The secret to co-creating with God is to choose to be the embodiment of Love, and then to play with and practice that embodiment. It is through co-creative service and love to others that we allow God to be within us, to mentor us, and to guide us. With each surrender to serving the Divine, by serving each other, God is revealed to us.

Dear Highest God, let all of me be the embodiment of Divine Love for whomever you place on my path... my friends, family, neighbors, and acquaintances.

In my own experience, the blessing of loving my friends and the world unconditionally, through the direct guidance of God, ultimately opened me to the gift of the Flower of Heaven. It was blossoming inside of me the whole time God was mentoring me today, as the sun passed through the sky and settled over the horizon. However, it was not until evening that the light of the Flower of Heaven was fully revealed and gifted to me.

I was in a state of Grace free from suffering and full of Love with my eyes open. Heaven, which is God, was in me and all around me.

Then a beautiful friend, I met only five months ago, walked by me with a white flower in her hand. She stopped to briefly share her gratitude for our friendship. Without knowing the state I was in, and without knowing what she was really doing or saying, she gently brushed my arms with the fragrant white flower and placed it in my left hand. She said, "Let that ground you."

It powerfully and practically grounded me. It grounded me in the dance and glory of the Divine right here and now. The Great Story-Weaver and Mentor moved this woman to speak those words and place the flower in my hand, to solidify a powerful revelation, to bring it into the everyday, and to understand the gift in relationship to the simple, powerful, subtle Love of God.

Her action was profoundly significant because in that moment that she placed the flower in my hand, God also kissed my consciousness, and the Flower of Heaven blossomed fully within me. **The Flower of Heaven is the Flower of Friendship.** My heart center filled with gratitude for friendship and for fellowship as we explore existence and creation from the unique experience of going from Light to Dark, and back to Light again. I knew in that moment that we are all inextricably linked to awaken together. My whole beingness was smiling.

Chapter 5 - Revelation

We are so lightly here.
It is in love that we are made.
In love we disappear.
~Leonard Cohen

Love exists. Out of Love, creation unfolds to respond to Love and embody the Love that created it. You are Love. You are invited to remember your True embodiment, to be the Light that shines in the darkness.

Simple, true, unconditional friendship allows the Flower of Heaven to reside within your heart and blossom within your consciousness.

Be a friend to all. The recognition of the beauty of the other is the recognition of God singing uniquely through each of you.

Let me share more about this Flower of Friendship that is so dear to God. We are placed here in this strange darkness, to come home to ourselves, to come home to God. The Divine has designed it exquisitely. We are to do it together.

My path is woven with others. The grace of friendship has awakened me. Each relationship I have encountered in this life, including the frenemies, adversaries, bullies, and narcissists, have all contributed to the awakening that is happening within me.

God did not reveal Truth to me to keep it for myself. The Divine is delighted to share Wisdom and Truth with you. To receive means to shine, to be the embodiment of Love. It cannot get bottled up. It has to go everywhere. Divine Truth comes easily to the generous; as it flows, more follows.

If you look at many images of Buddhas, Christ, or saints from various traditions, you will see an open hand, like a cup, receiving Grace and an open hand facing out to the world, blessing the world with Grace. I know this because I experienced the Truth of these images before my friend gave me the flower. When I write of grace with a small *g*, I am referring to everyday Divine blessings like food, water, friendship, family and safety. When I use Grace with a capital *G*, I am referring to Divine blessings such as the power to heal another, to receive Truth, and to know who you are.

Unlike the old photo of me as the Green Tara, where I had a mental understanding of the images of holy beings to some degree, today the awakening of God's Grace moved me into those sacred mudras for hours.

I AM the revelation, the embodiment of the blessing, and the wisdom of receiving and giving Divine Grace.

Throughout the day, I was mentored in True Friendship.

Then in the evening, once my friend gifted the white flower to me, I was both holding the Flower of Heaven in my left hand and in my whole beingness as the blessings of Grace revealed the Divine

62

blessings of friendship. Simultaneously, the blessings flowed out of my right hand. I had become the embodiment of compassion, and here I sat as Tara Bianca, the White Tara. Traditionally she is known for her compassion, serenity, longevity, and healing.

God then revealed the song of the names of people I personally knew who were suffering deeply. I asked the Divine for forgiveness for any and all suffering I have created in this lifetime or beyond, and I asked for forgiveness on behalf of those people for their actions. I surrendered to the Divine on behalf of those who are in the darkness stage. I asked that the Light of Healing and Truth be upon them.

The Creator simply told me, *"Love them."*

Me loving them allows for healing. You loving others allows for healing. Healing at the deepest level means to be witnessed no matter what one experiences, to be loved no matter what one has done or no matter how lost one feels. It is the hand that reaches out to the person who is drowning. It is the light upon the dark cellar of the lies that the mind collects. God says, *"No matter what, Love is a witness of you."*

I heard their names spoken by the Divine. God is with them, sees them, and loves them. I see them and love them. They are not forgotten. They are remembered.

Then God sang my name. I was born with the name Tara Bianca. In Sanskrit, the language of ancient India, Tara means 'star' or 'to cross over the ocean.' Bianca in Italian means 'white, shining.' What a blessing to me to be born with such an evocative name as

Star Shining White. When God sang my name, it was the revelation of Truth of the greater 'me,' which is We. The song revealed, White Star Flower, Shining Upon All. It is the song of God's blessing upon you when I surrender to the Truth of Divine Friendship in me.

The opportunity to open deeply to God can develop by being a Divine blessing for others. How exciting! I love it!! I love that we are all connected. Not one being is left behind. We do it together.

I choose love. I choose friendship.

Throughout my life, it has been my experience that every time I serve another, I am blessed. Every time I gaze into the eyes of another, I am blessed. Every time I access unconditional love for another, I am blessed. Every time I hug someone, I am blessed. Every time I unconditionally hold space for another's suffering, I am blessed. I am blessed to serve you.

So here, I share with you, by the Grace of God, I AM Loving <u>You</u>!

Why is it so empowering to choose love?
Why is it so joyful to open my heart to love?

Part II - Action

I am the owner of my actions, heir to my actions, born of my actions, related through my actions, and have my actions as my arbitrator. Whatever I do, for good or for evil, to that will I fall heir.
~ Anguttara Nikaya 5.57

Chapter 6
The Blessings of Friendship

Whatever we are we belong together.
Wherever we are, we will find each other.
Whoever we are we are forever one.
~Leonard Nimoy

Unconditional loving friendship is the foundation for all relationships. Given the amount of suffering around the world, opening to unconditional, loving friendship is an action we can choose for improving the physical and mental well-being of ourselves and others. Loving friendship is also a way to explore a meaningful life, to contribute to more cohesive and loving communities, to learn about ourselves, to cultivate love within ourselves, to expand our consciousness, and to deepen our connection with the Divine.

The Loneliness Epidemic

I may indicate briefly what to me constitutes the essence of the crisis in our time. It concerns the relationship of the individual to society... [A person's] position in society is such that the egotistical drives of his make-up are constantly being accentuated, while his social drives, which are by nature weaker, progressively deteriorate. All human beings, whatever their position in society, are suffering from this process of deterioration.

Unknowingly prisoners of their own egotism, they feel insecure, lonely, and deprived of the naive, simple and unsophisticated enjoyment of life. Man can find meaning in life, short and perilous as it is, only through devoting himself to society. The economic anarchy of capitalist society as it exists today is, in my opinion, the real source of evil.

~ Albert Einstein, 1949

Friendship and loving connection are absolutely needed right now. If you look around your friend base or in your community, you may be aware of a great disconnection within most people. How is it that we are more connected worldwide than ever through social media, but people feel lonelier and more isolated than ever before?

To get a clear sense of where we need to collectively go, we need to know where we are.

Depression and anxiety affect people around the world. According to the World Health Organization, 300 million people around the world have depression. Humanity is suffering in large numbers. Disconnection and loneliness contribute to depression, but depression also leads to further isolation and disconnection. It becomes a cycle of hopelessness for many people.

The number one issue most of my clients come to me for is disconnection combined with the fear of not being good enough for connection. They feel a sense of hopelessness and helplessness about their disconnection.

The statistics are staggering. Americans are now faced with an epidemic of disconnection. Over 40% of US citizens feel alone. It is not just the elderly who experience loneliness; one study found that

48% of young adults born between 1995 and the early 2000's reported feeling lonely. The study also revealed that 39% of people over 72 years old felt lonely.[14]

The UK has appointed a Minister of Loneliness to address the country's growing issue with loneliness. Thirteen percent of people in the UK report that they have no friends. One in five shared that they feel unloved. At work, 42% of people have no work friends. At home, 43% of people living together feel lonely often or most of the time.[15]

Loneliness is also a serious issue in Japan where 30% of its citizens report having experienced loneliness for over a decade.[16] Japan faces elder lonely deaths at alarming rates, where a significant number of elders die alone and are undiscovered for a long period of time.

In addition, a growing number of people under 40 are not interested in conventional relationships due to work pressures, social conventions of both sexes, and the high cost of living. 30% of single Japanese men and women under 30 years old report never having dated. Many young Japanese professionals do not see the point of love, marriage, and parenthood.[17] [18]

The majority of my adult clients have come to me experiencing profound loneliness. At the root of their concern is profound aloneness they experienced as children, due to parents who were either emotionally unavailable or were too busy to connect. What we experience as children becomes familiar and we are more likely to replicate experiences and attract people who carry similar patterns as our primary care givers.

Perception vs. Actual

Although a person may be married, physically surrounded by a group of people or have a large group of friends, it does not mean they feel connected and fulfilled socially. If there is a lack of intimacy, bonding, or presence, a person can still feel lonely in the midst of a relationship.

How one perceives their social status, or the quality of their relationships, affects people's feelings of loneliness and is identified to significantly increase mortality by 26%.

With so much growing isolation and disconnection in many developed nations, a major shift in consciousness is imperative. To end the cycle of generational loneliness, new parents need to make connecting familiar and to set boundaries around technology for all family members. It is unfortunate to see toddlers on devices when out with their parents, rather than interacting with them. Equally disconnecting is a parent who is on their device when they are out for a walk with their child. What is happening at home? I see the future of psychology orienting around teaching individuals, couples, and families how to be present and connect with each other in nourishing ways.

Health Risks

A lack of social connections and loneliness increases the risk for premature mortality considerably and is comparable with the risks associated with obesity and substance abuse.[19] Isolation and loneliness jeopardize longevity as much as smoking 15 cigarettes a day or being an alcoholic. A Harvard study found that middle aged

70

adults who live alone have a 24% greater risk of dying of heart disease. Across research, actual social isolation also increases the risk of death by 29%. Living alone increases mortality risk by 32%.

Loneliness also strains the immune system. Chronically high levels of loneliness can adversely affect the immune system by triggering inflammation, and can lower antiviral response and antibody production.[20] [21]

In a retirement study, accelerated cognitive decline in people 65 and older was linked with the social and emotional distress of loneliness.[22]

Research also reveals that people who reported having strained relationships were more likely to experience higher levels of stress, mental health concerns, and health issues.

Benefits of Friendship

A good friend is a connection to life
— a tie to the past, a road to the future,
the key to sanity in a totally insane world.
~ Lois Wyse

Establishing, creating, or deepening conscious friendship is a blessing to you, your friends, and the world. Every act of love for others contributes to the restoration of the Holy brilliance of you. The blessing of extending unconditional friendship to another or cultivating meaningful, loving relationships with your friends is that as you nourish another in friendship, you also are nourished.

When you cultivate quality relationships, not only do you feel better and help your friends feel better, but you contribute to an increase of joy, love, and peace in the world.

When you cultivate peace within yourself, your mental, emotional, physical, and spiritual well-being increases. When you embody peace, you infuse the world with peace.

Attuning oneself to conscious friendship with the world is an action-based way to begin to heal loneliness and move into connection.

Friendship can seem like a simple concept. One might reflect, "I am a good friend. I do nice things for people. I support charities or good causes."

I am inviting you into a deeper level of friendship, to bring conscious awareness, choice, and growth into your relationships. For children the openness to friendship is natural. Children always have time for friends. It is not even a choice for most kids, it is an intrinsic delight. A play date! Yay, I get to go play with my friends! When they have to go home, they lament and kick up a fuss. Children love creating, cultivating, exploring and celebrating friendship.

For adults, friendship requires choice. As people get older and busier with work and family responsibilities, they often put friendship on the back burner or simply put off time with friends until they are less busy. Life sees the vacuum and seems to fill up your calendar anyway. You choose what you invest in, so choose wisely. Friendship is essential to your mental, physical, and emotional health, self-esteem, longevity, work, community and the world.

When we put off nurturing our most important relationships, they wither. Our relationships need consistent watering just like plants. If a plant goes without water for long enough, it will die: and there is no bringing it back.

If you have children or a spouse, you need to connect with them one-on-one every day. To nurture your connections, hug your family members daily, have conversations, and share loving, supportive and positive things about each other. Sharing a meal as a family without electronic devices, doing a group activity such as a walk or a weekly excursion is paramount to establish connection.

It is not a lack of love, but a lack of friendship
that makes unhappy marriages.
~ Friedrich Nietzsche

For friendships, sending loving text messages or having brief phone conversations to maintain intimacy is helpful when busy, but making time to physically visit with friends is vital. If you have kids and time is short, invite a friend over to have dinner with you and your family or to walk with you and your kids.

Life is about many things, and fun is one of them. Fun experiences release stress, nourish us deeply, strengthen our connections and elevate everyone involved.

How can you make sure to schedule fun times with your friends and family? What joyful and connecting experiences can you create this week? Make connecting a priority and an intrinsic value in your life.

Improved Health

Researchers have observed that general health is improved through social interactions. It is enhanced even more when our relationships are based on love and support. Having strong social connections relaxes the nervous system, improves cognitive functioning, strengthens the immune system, reduces stress,[23] and anxiety, reduces the impact of emotional pain, reduces the intensity of physical pain, and increases longevity.

The **quantity** of our friendships plays a role in our health. Studies have found that social capital through friendships can improve health. Just adding one friend can increase a person's health measure by 6.6%.[24]

The **quality** of our relationships is more important than the number of friends we collect when it comes to improved health and a greater sense of satisfaction in life.[25] Having friends who are accepting, supportive, available, and loving are key to feeling safe. If you choose to cultivate better friendships, begin by being a great friend to others.

The **frequency** of our interactions with friends is also key. If you do not have time to spend with your friends, the depth of your friendships can be affected and bonds may not be as strong, as relationships stay shallow. Friendships, like flowers, require consistent watering. Quality of life increases as the quality of our friendships increase.

More Fulfilling & Peaceful Work Environments

It turns out that our brains are literally hardwired to perform at their best not when they are negative or even neutral, but when they are positive. Yet in today's world, we ironically sacrifice happiness for success only to lower our brain's success rates.
~ Shawn Anchor

The average person spends at least eight hours a day in the workplace. That equates to over half of the waking hours of one's weekday. So, our sense of connection and community at work is just as important as our personal time. Studies have found that long-term work relationships with strong bonds reduce work-related stress.[26] As an employee, create simple ways to connect with your fellow employees. If you own a business or are an influencer at work, think about ways your workplace can assist its employees to bond. Providing comfortable collaboration spaces, organizing off-site company-sponsored lunches or events, and leading creative team building activities are all great ways to improve productivity, collaboration, communication, creativity, and motivation. It also encourages communication and allows for employees to build trust by getting to know each other.

Increased Longevity & Happiness

Numerous studies have established that cultivating social interactions, connectivity, and a strong friendship base is essential for longevity and happiness. Loving, fun, safe relationships are the foundation and greatest predictor of health and happiness in life. When we feel connected our immune system functions better, mood improves, stress levels decline, overall health improves, and we experience a higher quality of life.

Specific regions throughout the world, called Blue Zones, have been identified where people live much longer than average. Shared characteristics of Blues Zones reveal that community, family, and strong social ties are among key factors that contribute to longevity and even the potential to live past 100 years.

What matters most to the wellness of a person is the quality of connections, feeling supported, and feeling safe enough to be vulnerable. Meaningful social interaction is key to reducing or eliminating loneliness. Getting out, socializing, meeting friends, being socially vulnerable with others, and bonding are critical to well-being.

Improves the Field & Lightens the World

A fundamental conclusion of the new physics also acknowledges that the observer creates the reality. As observers we are personally involved with the creation of our own reality.
~ Richard Conn Henry

In this one cosmos, as part of the family of humanity, in our beautiful, resplendent Universe, we dance through this life interconnected. I am affected by you and you are affected by me. Our environments, from the micro to the macro, affect our mood, beliefs, and consciousness. When you are in a personal coherent state, where unconditional loving friendship radiates from your heart center, those around you benefit in subtle and powerful ways. You are improving the field of creation, not only one friendship at a time but your powerful loving radiance permeates all of existence. You have the power to up-level your energy and consciousness, but also to uplift those around you and beyond. You influence your surroundings by every thought, emotion, word and action.

It is important to note that knowing this does not mean that you have to be perfect, nor does it mean that you should feel guilty or judge yourself if you do not attain optimal coherence. We all go through states where we are emotionally and mentally challenged. The key is to notice when you lose your Love state and to return to it by healing whatever is blocking you from being attuned to the power of you.

Learning how to both be free of the influence of others and to free others from your influence is important when you or others are resonating in a low state.

Action Based Influence

You can make more friends in two months by becoming interested in other people than you can in two years by trying to get other people interested in you.
~ Dale Carnegie

A smile, a hug, or the warmth of your voice has an effect on everyone around you. Many experiments on kindness, whether in the workplace, among friends, or between strangers, reveal that acts of kindness boost happiness for both the receiver and the giver, and decrease depression. In some cases, acts of kindness can affect those receiving them so deeply, that it gives them hope where none existed before. Acts of kindness at any age leave people with a sense of being cared for and often end up being contagious.[27] [28] [29] [30]

In attachment theory studies, researchers have observed that children are highly susceptible to both the emotional states and actions of their caregivers and that interpersonal patterns between children and their caregivers can last a lifetime. The more emotionally available a caregiver, the greater the sense of safety in a child. This leads to a familiarity with healthy relationships. On the flipside, when caregivers are not emotionally available or the emotional needs of a child are sporadically met, a child becomes familiar with love not being available. This has a strong effect on how a child relates to others and the world.[31]

Think how the effect of a harsh word or action puts people into a contracted state by imagining a mother yelling at a young child and swinging to hit them. How does this make your body, mind, and energy feel?

Now think of how a kind word or loving action puts others at ease and creates a field of relaxation and acceptance by imagining a mother saying to her child as she hugs them, "I'm so proud of you." How does this image make your body, mind, and energy feel?

You can extend this thought experiment to any relationship dynamic at home or at work to notice the power of positive actions. Supportive, mentoring, and loving actions are powerful ways to help others to regulate their emotions and to have a positive effect on the field of life. Wonderfully, when you assist others to regulate their emotions, it can also have a beneficial effect on regulating your emotions and decreasing symptoms of depression.[32]

Emotional and Energetic Influence

Think about a time when you have been around a sad, depressed, or angry person. How did it make you feel? Now think about how you feel when you are around joyful, peaceful, loving people. And how do you feel right now thinking about positive, peaceful people?

We know how it feels to be around a joyful versus an angry person. Emotional states can be transferred directly from one individual to another by many factors, and over varying periods of time and can even be passed through online social networks. How you feel has the potential to influence others and how others feel can potentially influence you.

When people are in an emotionally close relationship with each other or have certain interests or beliefs connecting them, positive or negative emotional states can be contagious.[33] A University of Zurich study observed how students' perception of their teachers' emotions are as significant as their instructional behavior on the students' emotions.[34] In another study, researchers found that students assigned to mildly depressed roommates became increasingly depressed over a period of three months.[35]

Many studies have established how positive and negative emotions can be transferred through social networks, both in person and online. In one experiment with users of Facebook, researchers tested emotional contagion in online settings by manipulating emotional content in the News Feed. They found that emotions can be transferred to others electronically.[36]

The stress of one person can also affect the physiology of another when there is resonance between the two people. Researchers have observed both an increase in cardiac activity and in stress hormones in those who observe another who is stressed.[37] [38] Conversely, when we individually and collectively increase our sense of well-being and reduce stress, it has a ripple effect radiating out to those around us.

In another study focused on small groups of people, researchers measured heart rate variability coherence (HRVC), which is the measurement of the body's ability to deal with stress. They observed the effects that small groups of three people with healthy HRV would have on the HRV of an individual with poor HRV. They found that the HRV of the individual with the poor HRV improved in approximately half of the individuals studied. When all four people focused on increasing HRV coherence, the rates were the highest. Another influencing factor for improved HRV coherence was higher levels of comfort between the participants. This study is a good example of how the intentions, comfort level, and proximity of healthy individuals can cultivate a coherent positive energy field.[39]

What happens at work if a group of employees' most basic needs are not met? How might that affect the company's environment on a day-to-day basis? If employees are dissatisfied, how does that affect their interaction with customers? When co-workers express gratitude to each other, or a company celebrates its employees, we know that employee relationships are strengthened and productivity increases, health and wellness improves, and people feel more relaxed and positive. How might that company's culture affect their own family members at home, their customers, or even the immediate community and beyond?

Personal healing can also influence your relationships in powerful ways. In my therapy practice, I have clients who have worked with me to heal childhood emotional conflicts. Many of them experience an interesting change in their field. When they next see their family, they find that their family members interact in healthier ways. When they return for follow-up sessions, they are curious and sometimes joke, "How did you change my parent/spouse/child?" Or they ask, "I know I changed but why did they change?"

I often share that when they completed the internal work and released the stories and lies within them, the other person was subconsciously released from the role they assigned them in their mind and no longer has to show up and play the role of the villain or be in that dynamic with them.

When you free yourself, you free others too. You are then clear to create something new with your loved ones. Also, when you stop having expectations of them to be different and have freed them from your influence, they do not need to energetically defend themselves and can now take responsibility for what is their responsibility.

As our inner field awakens to Truth, we radiate that out into the world. We resonate with others who are awakening, and the field of existence begins to reflect our collective inner awakenings.

Love activism is key to changing the overall field of creation from suffering to peace. When we are aware of people suffering in other nations or human-made environmental atrocities, how does that affect our mood? How amazing would we feel if we actually helped solve environmental, economic and social issues? How joyful would we feel knowing that the oceans were cleaned up of heavy metals and plastic? How satisfying would it feel to know that people who were starving were fed? How loved would people feel if they were fed, clothed and cared for?

Why is it so easy to make new friends?
Why is it so joyful to uplift others with kind words and actions?
Why is it so peaceful to lovingly support my friends and family?

Why is it so lovely to open my heart to loving,
supportive friendships?

Chapter 7 - Sacred Relationships

*What you do not want done to yourself,
do not do to others. ~ Confucius*

*Precious like jewels are the minds of all.
To hurt them is not at all good.
If thou desirest thy Beloved,
then hurt thou not anyone's heart.
~Guru Arjan Dev Ji*

All relationships are sacred because we are all connected. Relationships are foundational to the survival of individuals, communities, nations, humanity, ecosystems, flora, and fauna. Life demonstrates sacred interconnectivity in various ways.

Interconnection of Nature

Everything is interconnected. This existence has been programmed to ensure all species and ecosystems rely on each other. More importantly, existence has been programmed so that humans rely on most other species.

Insects are an example of essential species for the functioning of all ecosystems and for the survival of the human race. There are over 900 thousand identified species of insects in the world. However, scientists believe that this number represents only 20% of the actual number of global species of insects.

Insects are fundamental for all ecosystems as they ensure pollination of fruits and vegetables, provide food for many species, recycle nutrients by breaking down decaying matter, and return nitrogen back to the soil when they die. Without insects to do this work for us, for all of existence, humans would not thrive, and life as we know it would change dramatically. Pollution, agricultural use of pesticides, herbicides, and fungicides, habitat changes due to deforestation and development, and climate change are contributing to major die-offs of insect populations.

The world's ocean fish stocks are also on the verge of collapse. The ocean ecosystems rely on us to keep them pristine and in balance, and we in turn rely on the health of the oceans. The current rate of global fishing is no longer sustainable. It has been reported that if the world continues fishing at its current rate, there will be no fish left by 2050.[40] If all nations continue to pollute and over fish the oceans causing the catastrophic collapse of ocean biodiversity, can the human species survive?

We are caretakers of our own garden. What we do to the garden of existence, we do to ourselves. This requires all nations to do their part to change policy and practices to protect ecosystems, as all ecosystems belong to each and every species whether they reside in them or not.

Social Interconnection

We are also caretakers of each other within our social ecosystems.

When a child is born, their family and community rejoice and celebrate the sacred rite of passage of that child. The merry recognition of a new soul emerging and gracing our lives is a profound experience. The birth of a baby is the beginning of a journey of discovery of who this new being is, what they will embody, and how they shall live in relationship with their family, peers, communities, and the environment.

The birth of a child is a sacred covenant between the Divine, the child, their parent(s), and humanity. This child does not belong to any one or two people. Although a baby's body is made from the shared DNA from its parents, the being that animates that body is a Divine soul gracing that particular family and community to be mentored lovingly until the day they are ready to step into the world on their own. Even then, mentorship continues in a new way for that adult child. A new baby is a holy being entrusted to the world. Each child is a blessing to the world, and humanity is responsible for that child.

One of the most powerful and sacred relationships an individual has is with their mother, even if it is marred by emotional conflicts, disfunction, or abandonment. After conception, a baby is carried by their mother for 40 weeks as her body nourishes and grows them. Pregnant mothers are often exhausted by what it physically takes to grow a baby, and at times mothers are left depleted as nutrients are used to grow whatever is on the physical developmental menu for that day. This is service.

Mothers do the best they can with the resources they have to provide a nurturing environment for their babies. Once a baby is born, mothers (and sometimes fathers or grandparents) are often the primary caregivers and rely on the father, family members, friends, and their community to collectively grow and mentor the child into adulthood, as well.

You are because of your mother. Before you could feed yourself, someone fed you. Before you could crawl, someone carried you. Rest into the service that your mother expressed to you, no matter how imperfect it may have seemed. Give yourself permission to retrieve and receive her Love. See her in your vision as the one who cared for you, cleaned up after you, fed you, and held you as a baby as much as life allowed her to at that time.

Remember, the illusion of life intrudes to distract and disconnect families; forgive the illusion. Forgive the missteps of your mother and father. Most parents did the best they could with the programming and suffering they embodied. Remember them in Love.

You are because of everyone and everything who has ever cared for you directly or indirectly… including your family, friends, ancestors, doctors, nurses, teachers, neighbors, city workers, politicians, gas station owners, and workers, petroleum companies, clothing manufacturers, farmers who have grown your food, truck drivers, store owners, animals, microbes, plants, rain, water ways, oceans, forests, wind, stars, and so many more people and elements. At all stages of life we need each other. All aspects of life contribute to each other. Each of us serves as a blessing to the other.

Humans need each other for emotional support, physical touch, learning, physical survival and safety, securing and developing resources, and exploring uncharted territories physically and spiritually. After physical survival, the most important element for growing a healthy, whole person is for them to know they are emotionally supported and unconditionally loved.

If parents do not have the financial option to stay at home to nurture their babies when they most need parental connection, what is going to happen to people's ability to feel loved and cared for? We need parents to care deeply for babies and young children throughout the day, not just for a hectic hour or two in the morning or at night, as those children are our future leaders and caretakers.

We also need farmers to grow and harvest our food. We need legislators to look out for our collective needs and safety. We need teachers to nurture and mentor our children.

We need corporations to respect and cultivate healthy work environments. If we are over-worked, over-taxed and financially stressed, how will that affect our collective mental, physical, and emotional health and well-being?

We need you. As a friend to the world, would you let others be bullied or neglected? Would you let others suffer in alienation and aloneness? Would you let your elected leaders destroy the beauty of Divine creation, which is here to serve us all?

The Brain & Body

The brain contains mirror neurons that researchers believe may assist in learning new skills, developing empathy, understanding the actions of others or even in learning language. Essentially, a mirror neuron is a nerve cell that communicates with other cells through synapses. Researchers have observed that mirror neurons in the human brain get activated in the same places whether a person performs an action or whether the person observes another performing that same action.

You may have noticed that when you have observed another person being abused, or made fun of, you feel uncomfortable or sad, or it may trigger your own fears and physical responses. This is also problematic when watching a movie, TV show, or a video game, as your mind codes the experience as your own, and the body feels the effects as though it is your experience.

The Mind

Any rules you apply to others your mind applies to you. Every time you accept that it is okay for another person to be made fun of or rejected socially, you are telling your mind it is okay for others to make fun of you and to reject you. The subconscious mind automatically applies the same rules to you as you do to others. This occurs even if you consciously believe making fun of you is unacceptable.

For example, take a group of children making fun of or rejecting a child who is overweight, or even standing by while others make fun of that child. If any of these children gain weight at any time in their lives, they will feel deep subconscious fear of rejection or shame for now being the one who has gained weight.

In another example, if a child grows up experiencing sadness for a lack of time spent with a father who works extremely long hours, they might apply the rule to their own mind that working at a job creates pain. When that child becomes an adult, they might find they have an unconscious resistance to working because of this unresolved conflict.

To heal deep, unconscious self-judgment and shame, begin by asking for forgiveness from those you have harmed or let be harmed. A powerful forgiveness practice, such as *Ho'oponopono* (Chapter 10), is a wonderful way to clear harmful and negative actions from the past. In addition, practice *Freedom from Influence* (Chapter 8) to free others and yourself from judgment and expectation.

The Soul

We are all one. Plain and simple. You may not yet have had this experience, but those who have entered into unity consciousness and have experienced oneness and connection with all of life, can attest to this. We are not only one with every person on the planet, but we are one with the whole field of creation. How we are with people, animals and nature affects us physically, mentally, emotionally, and energetically at a deep level and at the core of who we are.

As a blessing to you, make being a conscious friend a familiar paradigm for yourself.

Conscious Friendship

You may say I'm a dreamer,
But I'm not the only one
I hope some day you'll join us
And the world will be as one.
– John Lennon

Conscious friendship is the gateway to Heaven on earth. By opening your heart to unconditional loving friendship and love activism you are nurturing and blossoming the Flower of Heaven in your heart center. Surrendering to friendship transforms your mind, body and energy, as well as your relationships to yourself, others, nature, and animals.

Remember that you are in a process of awakening. As the Flower of Heaven is firmly rooted within you, the beauty of the Love that you are shines out for all and blesses you and the world, and awakens Love within others.

Being a conscious friend is about staying connected to the power and beauty of you while you are in relationship with others. It means being committed to keeping your heart open, even when it is challenging to do so, by remembering the Truth of your power and beauty. By keeping an open heart, you free the other from your influence, which means they do not have to be or do anything to make you feel okay about life.

How can I stay in the power of me?

It is the undirected mind that wants to judge, expect, or make you, others, or situations wrong. When you allow and go into negative thinking, you get caught up in these negative fantasies and you lose yourself. Always return to the love and peace that radiate from your heart center. It is essential to be clear with your mind about what you expect from it, in a loving way.

Having a clear intention and vision of what you choose to embody is fundamental to staying in your power, cultivating presence, and being a conscious friend. Establish a key attribute to embody: love, connection, freedom, awareness, peace, or joy. Keep it simple and easy to recall.

Always have your embodiment in mind when interacting with others, especially when faced with relationship challenges, such as when the other person shuts down or gets lost in the illusion. You can do this by having the word posted on a wall, the fridge, or your screensaver. There are also stones you can buy engraved with these types of words that you can place on your desk at work as a reminder.

If you get pulled into the mind, use the word as a cue to recall your chosen embodiment. Then return back to feeling that attribute from the heart center. For example, if you choose to remember the virtue or embodiment of *peace*, when someone gets angry with you at work, bring your awareness to your heart centre and establish or anchor peace there. Choose it, feel it, and ask, "What would peace do in this circumstance?"

You choose to either give up peace or establish peace. If it should happen that you lose peace to someone else's anger, be gentle with yourself; simply be accepting and return home to peace once again. Keep choosing to rest into peace. In addition, celebrate when the mind takes you into positive states, such as peace, compassion, love, and joy. You can literally praise your mind by saying, "I feel so empowered when I feel peaceful" or "Thanks, mind, for helping me stay peaceful."

What if I get my heart broken?

And the day came when the risk to remain tight in a bud
was more painful than the risk it took to blossom.
~ Anais Nin

Being a conscious friend does not mean that you will feel happy all the time. At times, you will encounter challenges with others or need to look at some vulnerable aspects within yourself, such as deep insecurities, negative patterns, wounds, and damaging beliefs. We all need to do this work to heal. This is known spiritually as a purification process. None of us are exempt from having to do this deeper work if we want to grow and experience the fullness that the Divine has created for us in this life. It is everyone's responsibility, whether they choose to step into their responsibility or not.

Deep work = deep awakening

Whatever comes up, resolve it. It is your responsibility and your opportunity. Being more vulnerable means you have the opportunity to heal and deepen into intimacy, and to feel free.

No matter what anyone says or does, how you feel is your choice and responsibility. This does not exempt the other from their own personal responsibility; actions have consequences. When you behave in hurtful ways, there are consequences. It could be a friendship ending, others not trusting you, or other people

92

suffering due to your actions. When others act in hurtful ways, you have a responsibility to take care of your needs and to assess whether it serves you to be in relationship with the other person. More importantly, it is your responsibility to not hurt yourself with the behavior, beliefs, or actions of other people.

Remember that people who behave in hurtful ways have been programmed sometime in their childhood to be that way. If they are willing to learn and grow with you, you can communicate how their behavior has affected you, as well as what your needs are. You can ask them if they are willing to meet your needs. If they say *no*, you can be curious and ask them *why*. Maybe they do not know how. Maybe they are just not willing. When you have a clear answer, you can more easily respond and choose for you.

The blessing is that we are designed to do this work together. We are all part of a greater mysterious game that goes faster and more peacefully when we do this deep work in relationship with each other. You are being invited into a shift of consciousness that will not only benefit yourself but will benefit the whole world. This love-shift, in how we view our emotional conflicts and how to resolve them with others, creates a safe haven for deep, transformational work. It allows us to move from stuck states to freedom, from wrongness to 'getting better' mindsets, and from fear of rejection to self-acceptance.

While remaining in the *power of you,* love the other as they are, look deep into your own wounds, and shine the light of awareness on any internal conflicts. This requires presence. Look with compassionate awareness as you gaze at your own vulnerabilities.

When we move through difficult emotions and illuminate false beliefs within us, beautiful healing, transformation, and deep intimacy bless us. The heaviness lifts and trust, peace, and gratitude wash over our experience. When we practice being present and conscious in our relationships, presence becomes familiar, we become more resourceful, and our potential expands.

Open your heart to the world without expectation. Just love people.

Love requires no reciprocation. It is a state of consciousness that sometimes has side effects, such as joy, lightness of being, peace, and sometimes bliss. At times the Love state feels neutral or equanimous. When a person feels neutral toward others, they may question whether they love someone, because they do not feel overwhelming passion or emotion. I often ask, "If this is romantic love and you do not feel big feelings, who do you most want to spend time with?" They say, "My partner of course." Sometimes you will simply feel peaceful and very comfortable with the person you deeply love, rather than excitement or passion.

Often people determine their self-esteem and worthiness of love based on whether they are in a romantic relationship or not. You are lovable if you are single. You are lovable even if someone breaks up with you, betrays you, or ignores you. To cultivate deep self-love that is not affected even when someone breaks up with you or distances themselves from you, learn to Love the world. When you see and love the beauty of the earth and the people throughout the globe, you enjoy the glow of consistent, ongoing joy, peace, and equanimity.

In addition, develop a foundational loving friend base. Among your close friends, be sure to choose emotionally available friends who are loving, generous, fun, light-hearted, loyal, and who are willing to be honest with you in clear, kind, loving ways. Surround yourself with loving mentors and people who care about others.

There are times when you will meet people who choose to be conscious friends, and times when others will shut down and walk away.

What do you do if someone else shuts down?

Let the other know you are there when they are ready and that you accept their decision. They may need to feel safe to come to the relationship. The other person may not feel they have the inner resources or communication tools to communicate effectively. They may not feel comfortable feeling anger, sadness, confusion, or frustration. Society, in general, has been operating from a protective, dysfunctional, and disconnected embodiment. We have become masters at avoiding feelings, challenges, and conflict through entertainment, sex, alcohol, drugs, and even extreme sports.

Over time, unresolved, painful emotional conflicts build within us. All those conflicts contributes to mounting stress within the mind and body. If the other is unavailable, then do your own work. Even if someone is not in your life anymore, you can heal anything that is unresolved. Chapter 9 offers tools for resolving emotional conflicts and difficult relationship dynamics.

Qualities of Conscious Friends

Be humble more than a blade of grass, more tolerant than a tree,
offering respect on to others and never expecting any in return.
~ Chaitanya Mahaprabhu

Conscious friendship is about being aware of, having knowledge of, being responsive to, and cultivating loving connection and friendship. Being a conscious friend is not about having to be a perfect friend or to have to be perfect in your actions. When I define conscious friendship or what it means to be a conscious or true friend, it is to point the way to an experience of friendship that blesses you and the world. Step by step, action by action, in your own timing you move toward your vision of being a loving friend.

Becoming more conscious and present in your relationships helps strengthen your relationships with friends, family and co-workers. A conscious friend is unconditionally loving, patient, present, gentle, clear, honest, and kind. It is with conscious friendship that we invite and nourish peace within our hearts and connect with others unconditionally.

A conscious friend allows for a balance between the influence of the heart, soul, and mind. They are heart centred in that they lead with the heart, attuning to what Love would do in all circumstances. They are soul centred in that they are aware of the deep significance of friendships in this life and beyond this life as Divine beings. Beyond this life, we are all connected in Love. It is also important to be practical both by guiding the mind to set and achieve our goals and to use the mind for understanding and discernment in our relationships.

Allow for the ebb and flow of relationships, as there is a season and a time for everything. Be forgiving of yourself and others. Loving friends are keen to resolve conflict and to learn skills to be resolution-oriented. When expressing your needs, be open and honest in respectful ways with others. Being honest about your needs is a true act of friendship, as repressing your needs to be more accepted (co-dependence) creates both suffering for you, and contributes to relationship drama in the long run.

Be willing to allow others to feel disappointed in your choices or even in you. Be willing to allow others to disapprove of you. Their disappointment has little to do with you, and more to do with their own expectations of how life and people should be. There is nothing wrong with people feeling disappointed in general, but to project disappointment onto another is about blame, and is an act of violence against the other person and the relationship. This is a multigenerational learned behavior and a way of manipulating others to conform to outdated rules and beliefs.

When others express disappointment in you, understand that although they may be trying to get you to change or feel bad in some way, it is not a conscious act within them. They are acting in ways they have been programmed to behave by those who have mentored them. To experience peace, stop participating in cycles of abuse and suffering. Free yourself from any blame and free them from blame. Have compassion for their illusory contracted state and stand in the power of you knowing you are allowed to choose your path in life without finding yourself or the other person wrong.

You may need to learn and grow from time to time; you might reflect and see how you could have handled situations better. However, when you react defensively or angrily to another person trying to make you wrong, you only strengthen the idea that you are intrinsically wrong. When you stand in the power of you, accepting and loving yourself, you can have compassion for the other. No matter how they are toward you, you can stand in the inherent rightness of you.

Allow yourself to experience disappointment without making the other person wrong. For example, if you make plans with a friend and they are unable to attend for important reasons, feeling disappointed is normal, as you may miss them and were looking forward to seeing them. However, being disappointed in them when circumstances demanded they change their schedule is misplaced and is an act of violence against both you and them.

Along your journey, lovingly accept wherever you are and grow from there. Accept others where they are too. Compassion comes from understanding that everyone, including you, is in the process of healing. The blessing of existence is that we are here to assist each other in healing our deepest wounds. We actually *need* each other to heal and to awaken spiritually.

A loving friend surrenders in service to the other when they need a listening ear, encouragement, space to figure things out, a shoulder to cry on, or some sobering advice. It may involve shining love upon the darkness when a friend is lost. This does not mean that you need to rescue people. Sometimes being in service means being a loving witness to the consequences of unhealthy choices a friend may make.

For example, if a friend keeps going back to the same unhealthy romantic partner over and over again, first free them to make whatever choices they make, even if they end up getting hurt. You can offer your honest advice lovingly, but free them to not have to act on it or hear it. Just support and love them each time.

At times it means taking a stand in love by choosing not to participate in actions that enable unhealthy behavior or cause suffering. For example, if you have a friend or family member who is a drug addict, giving them money is not a helpful act of service. Instead let them know you love them and you are there to assist them to find help when they are ready. If they lash out verbally or try to manipulate you by projecting guilt, have compassion and refrain from taking anything they say personally. Continue to stay in your loving power and let them experience their lost state. Be there to assist them when they are truly ready to receive help.

Sometimes when another person chooses a difficult path of suffering, we have difficulty with it because we do not understand it. That confusion feels uncomfortable and we want the situation resolved. We might think that to resolve the conflict within ourselves, we need the other person to be healthy or to make better decisions, so that we feel better.

The truth is, the conflict is within you and needs to be resolved there. To resolve the confusion, always return to the knowing that everyone gets to choose their journey in life. You do not need to understand why they choose their path. But to give you some insight, people choose suffering because they have unresolved conflicts within themselves: fear of rejection, not believing they are lovable, and thinking they are not worthy of life. Have compassion for them and free yourself from not having to resolve their conflict.

You can still be a loving witness to the other person from a distance. Sometimes we need to consider that we might be in the way of someone's journey toward healing and wholeness. We may need to get out of the way so the right person can step in, or so they can find their own Divinely led path to healing. Sometimes we need to let people simply choose their path for themselves including choosing a life of suffering. Love them even if they choose a path of suffering.

As a conscious friend you hold the field for your friends. Holding the field is about accepting them as they are, as the unique expression of their personality, just as they are. It allows you to let go of expectation that another person should be as you would like them to be. It empowers you to surrender to the freedom of non-judgment and peace.

You have the opportunity to free the other person from your influence and to free yourself from a judgmental mind. As you free the other, you free yourself from self-judgment and ideas of wrongness.

Conscious friendships are open, loving and typically harmonious because of the determination and focus each side places on resolving conflicts and cultivating harmony even when unseen conflicts and challenges occur with a friend. The key is to create a respectful environment for discussion and to learn helpful non-violent communication and interpersonal skills for resolution with a win-win mindset.

This willingness comes from a deep commitment to heal, to know oneself, and to be the witness to the healing and revelation that the other person experiences.

Establish trust and demonstrate loving friendship by never tearing another person down, not participating in talking behind another's back, nor revealing personal information about others.

Let any challenges be gateways to freedom. Let go of blame. Instead take responsibility for any and all of your emotions and actions, as everyone is a mirror to reveal to you what is longing to be healed within you. Personal growth and self-inquiry are cornerstones of being a conscious friend.

When you are triggered by an interaction with a friend, take responsibility and look at the emotional conflict within yourself without blaming you or the other person. When a friend is triggered in anger or hurt and we refrain from becoming defensive or taking things personally, the other can begin to shine light on their emotional conflicts.

Friendships are imperfect and dynamic. The blessings of friendship occur throughout the lifelong journey of that friendship. Although we can have amazing moments of joy and adventure with friends, the long-term weaving of friendship creates a beautiful tapestry of intimacy and growth. During relationship ups and downs, be open to accepting that relationships and people are not perfect. Let go of expectations. Free your friends to make mistakes, to be vulnerable, to have differing points of view, to trigger you and to be loved anyway. Always hold the vision for peace, joy, healing, growth and unconditional love in your relationships.

Be a consistent and an active friend reaching out to them to offer opportunities for fun connection or support when needed. A conscious friend celebrates the beauty, successes, and joys of their friends.

If you look back on your life, much of your growth and learning in life occurred with friends. Everyone you have encountered in life, especially your family and friends, contributed to your life and who you are right now. A dear friend reflected recently that all moments of significant change in her life involved friends.

Would you describe yourself as a conscious friend?

How could you develop more skills to be a conscious friend?

Surrendering to the Flower of Heaven

Friendship is the only cement that
will ever hold the world together.
~ Woodrow T. Wilson

The Divine is inviting you to be a friend to yourself, friends, family, humankind, fish, birds, animals, water, plants, and minerals. We are the caretakers of this world and each other. The Divine has entrusted the field of creation to us. It is your choice to surrender to the Flower of Heaven through love activism, or not. Surrendering to loving friendship is a gift for you to awaken the radiant Divine heart of love that exists within you. There are three steps to surrendering to the Flower of Heaven.

1. Choice - The first step of surrendering to the Flower of Heaven is choice.

You choose what you will allow in your heart and what you will create in this world. The Divine has given you free will.

Do you value love and connection? You are capable of being that which you would like to experience in this lifetime. If you are willing to allow yourself to be guided by unconditional love, be crystal clear with your choice. You can declare any of the following:

- I choose to surrender to the Flower of Heaven and allow it to guide my relationships.
- I choose to surrender to love, connection and friendship.
- I choose to surrender to loving the world unconditionally.
- I choose to surrender to love as my guiding principle in all that I am.
- I choose to surrender to Divine friendship, loving, and accepting everyone as they are.
- I choose to free the world from my influence and respect everyone's right to choose their path.

2. Action - The next step is to surrender to love activism and the wisdom of connection by taking loving action.

After choosing the Flower of Heaven, let your actions be guided by Love. Be connection. Be love. First offer Love to the world. How can you nurture the flower of loving friendship in the world?

Start with your current friends and loved ones. You never have to be perfect; none of us are. But you can practice every day. Just like any other skill, it takes step-by-step consistent practice. Some estimations suggest it takes 10,000 hours to master something, but of course natural skills and Divine Grace factor in too. If you practice loving everyone you meet throughout your day, each and every day, for the next two years, you will transform your consciousness and your life. If you practice even half of the day, you will make amazing progress. If you feel blocked or run into issues, use some of the tools in this book to heal them. It is okay to make mistakes and stumble; be gentle with yourself, then get back to being loving.

Unlike any other skill, when the Flower of Heaven blossoms fully in your heart and love activism becomes your embodiment you are changed in powerful ways that positively affect every aspect of your life and every interaction with others.

It helps to surround yourself with other love activists, loving friends, and inspiring mentors. Joining a tribe of love activists, participating in joyful activities, reading books or listening to talks by activists, change makers, and those who are connected to the Divine, reading sacred texts, singing inspirational songs, listening to uplifting music, and meditating helps nurture and inspire you to connect in loving ways with the world.

On a personal level recognize, celebrate, and support your friends and family, especially those who need it most in your immediate circle. Also establish a loving, connected friendship base with loving, supportive, kind friends to ensure you are being nurtured.

On a community level, together with your friends or family, contribute loving care to those most in need. This could be in the form of unofficially adopting an elder, mentoring a disadvantaged child, assisting community-oriented organizations, volunteering, changing the way a public organization operates or affecting local policy.

On a state or national level, get involved to effect policy changes and legislation for social equality, maternity support, health care, the environment, and elder care.

On a global level, recognize, celebrate and support change makers and organizations that are identifying issues and creating effective models to change things.

If you are in a position to love, support, protect, donate, resolve, innovate, help, steer, or educate, then do so.

What skills and actions can you bring to overcome personal, community, or global challenges for you, your family and friends, and for your brothers and sisters worldwide?

Let yourself be a gift of love and presence. The greatest gift you can offer the world is the gift of your presence as an unconditional observer and lover of the world. All acts of friendship are welcome.

3. Allowing - With each loving interaction with the world, let yourself feel the joyful radiance of Love.

Celebrate and honor all that you gift to the world. Allow yourself to feel the nourishing joy, peace and love of serving the world in loving ways. Rest into the joy of service. When you allow yourself to celebrate your act of service and your choice to be a loving friend and to actively love the world, you are nourished rather than depleted of energy. Let yourself rest in the beauty of your loving acts, in the beauty of those you serve, and in the beauty of life itself, as you serve the world.

Teach people to really receive your offering of love by never expecting thanks or remembrance. Let their joy be their expression of gratitude. For example, when a child receives a present and is filled with joy, we often interrupt their celebration by engaging their mind to offer verbal thanks to the other person. We are effectively teaching them to exit the pure joy state to pacify the other's need for validation through appreciation, which is societal programming. However, that child was naturally embodying gratitude. Can it be enough to drink from their embodiment and celebrate their joy joyfully within ourselves?

If your purpose is in alignment with Love, you are nourished as you serve. If it is in alignment with the ego mind and belief, then you can exhaust yourself. Let go of the belief that you are doing anything. Let the Divine love the world through you. If others offer gratitude, remind them that it is the Grace-force of the Divine merely moving through you to offer what is needed in that moment.

Stop looking to others for nourishment or rest, it is God's to give.

All rest happens in God.
All nourishment is dispensed by God.
All healing happens in God.

If you feel depleted and need rest because you have been giving and operating from a 'doing' mindset, let yourself first rest in and receive the beauty and nourishment of God's Love, accepting yourself as you are, as Divine creation.

Praying, meditation, dedicating your actions, surrendering your fears, asking for guidance, taking time to daydream, walking in nature, devotional singing, staying in present moment mindfulness, and hanging with God in all experiences are ways to rest in the Divine. As all nourishment is dispensed by God, allowing others to support you and care for you allows the Divine to nourish you through them. You bless others when you receive nourishment with gratitude and recognize their loving service as the Divine serving you. Let the Divine love you through the world.

Also important are receiving Divine nourishment by eating nourishing nutrient dense whole foods, gazing at the beauty of nature, and getting adequate sleep at night. God created the nighttime for humans to sleep for detoxing, balancing and healing all systems, organs, and cells. Think about sleep as the state we surrender into for healing and restoration.

It is optional whether you receive or not. You can stay in poverty or allow the nourishment of Love. Resting into the Divine is an act of surrender that can only occur with your clear and free will. To those who receive, more is given. Once rested in the Divine and you feel nourished, let yourself practice the sacred balance of sharing, which is simultaneous receiving and giving Love.

When you rest into the sacred balance you feel joyous and peaceful, your body, mind and energies become optimally balanced and you become the embodiment of Love.

Why is it so joyful to rest into the Love of God?

Why is it so freeing to surrender to and share the nourishment of God?

Acts of Kindness, Songs of Love

God does not require us to succeed;
he only requires that you try.
~ Mother Teresa

Be a loving activist in the world. We cannot wait for others, especially world leaders or the media, to bring about change. We must be a part of the change. I know you. You are Love. You can effect change with your loving heart. All acts of love are meaningful to those who receive them. However small an action, love can bring about meaningful change. When we all connect in this way, the world powerfully transforms.

The key is to listen to your heart, and open and surrender to the call of Love in your interactions with others. Start with your closest relationships and spiral out into the world. Follow the unique path of how Love is expressed through you. Love the world and serve the world in a way that is nourishing and sustainable to you. There is no need to exhaust yourself or to take on the weight of the world. You are not responsible for the suffering of the world. Have compassion when you know others are suffering, and stay in the power of you so that you may serve the world in effective ways that you are guided to serve lovingly. All service is nourishing when it is led by the heart, so feel into your love for the world.

Here is a short list of acts of kindness that allow you to sing the song of love to the world. This list is meant to inspire you to think of how you can serve your community or the world. Love others in ways that bring you joy and that are within your means. This is not a to-do list. Begin with one or two powerful, simple acts. Experiment and have fun loving the world.

- Smile to your heart, smile to the world.
- Be gentle with yourself.
- Be gentle with each and every person you meet.
- Adopt a child, a senior, a pet, or an environmental cause,
- Be a foster parent to a child,
- Volunteer to serve the neediest in your community,
- Donate to organizations that are making a difference to needy people and the environment,
- Lobby for environmental protection,
- Lobby for improved senior care facilities,
- Volunteer to be a mentor to a disadvantaged child,
- Befriend and mentor an immigrant or immigrant family,
- Sponsor a refugee,
- Investigate and let go of biases and stereotypes,
- Foster a foreign child, family, or community,
- Financially support loving causes and work in the world,
- Re-wild natural spaces in your community for wildlife,
- Help protect the natural world in your community, or
- Help protect the natural world in key places like oceans or forests, such as the Amazon. *

* Did you know that there are Indigenous Guardians all over the earth who are protecting your birthright and the birthright of future generations? The Amazon rainforest has been severely deforested, and its indigenous protectors have been violently harassed and sometimes murdered. They face encroaching devastation on all sides. They have no money or political influence to stop the industrial agribusiness complex. They feel alone and discouraged. Many are moved to suicide. They need your awareness, encouragement, friendship, political influence, and financial support to continue to protect sacred forests and natural places.

Friendship Circles

Gather your friends and invite them to co-create a circle of connection on 4 levels with:

- your immediate friendship with them,
- their family,
- your shared community, and
- the world.

Activate each other. Discover common interests for being a friend to the world. Offer acts of kindness, together, for those most in need. It is a great way to connect with each other, to deepen your bonds, and it is a fun way to tackle larger issues in the world.

Establish a circle within your friendship group. This could easily just be you and another person, or it can be a group of 6 or less. Invite each of them into a bond of love, loyalty, devotion, fun, service, and connection. You can have a ceremony with dessert, candles, and music. Celebrate each other. You can name your circle of friends, establish the vision for your group, and have guidelines for loving friendship. Be there for each other through blessings, celebrations, challenges, heart aches, sweat, and tears. Serve each other. Express gratitude and love for each other. Uplift each other. Create a safe space to explore the journey of life together.

You can establish a meditation or peace circle to radiate loving kindness and heart coherence to your community. You can also join existing prayer or meditation groups offline or online. Feel free to start a *Flower of Heaven Love Activist* Facebook community group in your town or city.

Activities to bond with your friendship circle in service to the world can include:

- Taking a dance or meditation class together,
- Organizing fun, nourishing events,
- Forming a weekly meditation group in person or online,
- Traveling to communities in the world that need assistance and lend a hand,
- Walking in the forest,
- Volunteering with each other,
- Addressing a global cause: social, environmental, political or economic,
- Sponsoring a child or children together,
- Connecting with other friendships circle somewhere in the world, or
- Starting a community friendship circle and invite others to participate.

The Secret Heart of this Book

The Divine asked me to place a gift here, in the heart of *The Flower of Heaven*, for those who were inspired to read this far. It is a blessing for your beautiful heart.

God designed and created you, and then gifted you to the world. You are a beautiful, glorious child of God.

May the illumination of God's Wisdom reveal your beauty to you. May your beauty nourish the world.

May the Flower of Heaven bless your heart, mind, and all levels of your being.

May the Flower of Heaven radiate out from your heart to bless the world.

I love you and know your Divinity and your ultimate destiny. It is ok if you have not yet realized who you are. You will know who you are, in the most perfect timing for you. For now, I invite you to open to the possibility.

Why is it so nourishing to receive the Flower of Heaven in my heart?

Chapter 8 – Nourishing Mindsets

A friend loves at all times. ~ Proverbs 17:17

The ego mind is a funny thing. It can often set people down a path of fearful misery. It can be challenging to open your heart to yourself or others in healthy ways when the mind is clouded in fear or psychological stress. Here are some powerful mindsets to help you ease and reframe the mind to open to conscious friendships to nourish the blossoming of the Flower of Heaven in your heart.

Playful Fun

In the sweetness of friendship let there be laughter,
for in the dew of little things the heart
finds its morning and is refreshed.
~ Khalil Gibran

Playful fun is one of the most foundational keys to nurturing friendship, developing intimacy, reducing stress and deeply nourishing you. Being relaxed and at ease within yourself through play and fun reduces stress and anxiety, increases productivity and makes you more magnetic.

Playfully celebrate beauty in any given moment. Present moment awareness is the key to experiencing the fullness and blessing of existence. There is so much beauty to celebrate in this life. Nothing is ever the same from moment to moment. Each day is a celebration. Each person is a blessing. Everything is a work of art. A pile of dishes, a pile of garbage, or a bouquet of flowers: there is beauty everywhere, if you have the stillness to see.

Include playfulness as a valued part of your personality. When you are playful, you naturally create the invitation for others to join in the fun and for them to feel relaxed and to connect with you in new ways. Playfulness opens your heart to friendship and love. As you choose to be playful you experience flexibility, openness, trust, and lightness of being.

Being playful is a mindset choice. Let go of the motto: 'work now, play later.' Let play be a part of your work, daily chores, and relationships, as well as the approach you take when interacting with life. Practice responding in playful ways with your family, friends, and coworkers. When you actively choose to make play a part of your everyday life, it eventually becomes a familiar behavior that reduces unnecessary stress and cultivates peace.

Allow yourself to be playful even in stressful or challenging times by letting yourself play and have fun with friends rather than putting it off until the external pressures are gone. You can also be lighthearted and laugh at stress circumstances or at your reactions to stress. This provides you with optimal energy and a mindset for new possibilities and solutions to flow into your life.

Let yourself be silly. Allow yourself to experience delight and to lovingly laugh at any mistakes you make. I used to be self-critical even if I tripped or dropped something. I was also highly critical when I made major mistakes. It was a subconscious behavior I learned from my father when he would express anger if I spilled milk or forgot to do something. I decided to change that behavior by laughing with myself and seeing myself as being goofy with small mistakes rather than judging myself as being wrong in someway. With major mistakes I am now naturally more accepting and loving with myself because my mind is familiar with relaxing with the small ones.

Choose to set aside time for surrendered fun with those you love. Organize fun activities and events. What do you have the most fun doing on your own or with others? Do more of that! If you have forgotten what fun you like to have, look back to your childhood or adolescence. What fun activities or connections brought you the most joy? Take new classes in areas of interest that you have always wanted to explore. Approach new activities with a playful, open mind without expectations, just to have fun and connect with others who are having fun. Invite your friends to try new activities with you.

If you have anxiety, control issues, or find it challenging to open your heart to have fun with other people, then attend improv classes or laughter yoga to assist you in opening up. Improv classes for people with anxiety are starting to become more available in North America. Improv aims to provide a judgment-free, safe and encouraging environment to play. The classes begin with trust building and exercises that help students let go of the internal critic. Even if you do not have improv classes for anxiety in your area, general improv classes can be just as helpful.

Laughter enhances overall well-being, alleviates stress, improves sleep, lowers anxiety and depression, fortifies the immune system, and more.[41] Laughter yoga is a great activity to reconnect you with laughter in a social setting. You may feel awkward the first time you attend but after a couple of classes you are more likely to feel incredibly relaxed and joyful.

Take vacations or local holidays, schedule in merrymaking and fun activities with your friends, laugh, smile, be silly, and remember to keep some time free to relax and for spontaneous fun.

In what ways can you integrate play into all you do?

Clarity & Intentional Manifestation

You are not the mind, at least not in the way that you think. The mind is a manifestation tool and it requires clear direction from you. If you do not instruct the mind, the mind creates your life based on whatever is stored within it: old outdated fears, protection programs, programming from society and a mix of beliefs based on past emotional conflicts and experiences. The mind wants to support you in the most effective and helpful way that it can, but cannot do so unless you are crystal clear about what you choose to create for your life.

If you would like to change your circumstances, you need to become more conscious and intentional about the life you would like to create. This means taking responsibility for the way your life is now, accepting it, and directing it to where you choose it to be. Being intentional is about you becoming curious, imagining possibilities, drawing from inspiration, choosing, and responding rather than being passive and reactive. For example, if your relationship with a loved one is disconnected and you would like for it to be more connected, try asking yourself positive questions to help shift your mindset about the relationship.

If you focus on the problem, you stay stuck in the problem. If you ask specific, open ended, positive questions that point to what you choose, you move in that direction because your mind is oriented to newness.

What is the most peaceful way to cultivate connection with my loved one?

What can I do to create connection?

The number one way to get your mind on board to manifest what you choose in life is to give it a clear map of your preferred attributes, experiences, goals, visions, and dreams. Be intentional about what you choose to experience in your relationships, community, recreational activities, health, learning, work, and income.

Intentional Life Mapping Exercise

Intentional Life Mapping can help you discover your preferences and intentions for your life, as well as to assist you to manifest those intentions to create the life you choose, instead of the one you do not want. When answering the following questions answer them as though you have all the resources and time you require to make each of them happen. Take 7 minutes for each question and quickly write as much as you can in that time. Be playful and allow yourself the freedom to be creative and to daydream about your future.

Step 1

What activities or experiences would you enjoy exploring in life? What would you like to learn? What skills would empower you? What new behaviors would you like to support within yourself? What would you like to embody or radiate to the world? Joy, fun, love, peace, freedom, acceptance, wisdom?

Step 2

Now, take your answers and write them out on a large piece of colored paper. When you write them out use present moment statements that begin with "I am" and a verb with 'ing.' For example, *I am peacefully living in a nourishing, beautiful home with bright natural light, and a backyard that has a vegetable garden*. If addressing your career you might write, *I am developing and teaching enriching programs to assist my students to feel confident as they transition into college*. For travel you might write something general or something specific, such as *I am joyfully travelling to Italy to learn more about the local customs and traditions of the smaller towns and seaside villages*. Here are some present moment verbs to inspire you to write your statements:

- I am enjoying….
- I am experiencing…
- I am teaching….
- I am travelling….

- I am learning….
- I am feeling empowered as I…
- I am celebrating….
- I am radiating…
- I am sharing…
- I am helping…
- I am allowing…

Step 3

At the end of your life, what big goals would you like to have achieved? What would you like to be remembered for? What contributions would you most like to have made?

Step 4

On a separate piece of paper, take your big goals and write out statements beginning with, "It excites, delights, and empowers me to…" If your big goal is to change the life of one person in a significant way, you might write: *It excites, delights, and empowers me to mentor a young person who needed guidance to fulfil their dreams.*

Step 5

Take both pieces of paper and place them on your wall. Every day or every few days, read your statements. Really feel what it would feel like if you were living your statements. Envision yourself high-fiving yourself and smile deeply when you think of each one.

Effective Communication

The first step in effective communication is getting clear about what your needs are. If you do not know what your needs and wants are, how can you express them to someone else?

The second step is to learn and apply effective communication skills, such as Non-Violent Communication (NVC). NVC is about heart centred, clear and peaceful communication. It offers a way for people to communicate their needs and to listen effectively without making the other person wrong, by expressing both your needs and offering a solution request. An example of expressing your need is, "When you forgot my birthday, I felt sad because I have a need to be celebrated on my birthday." The solution request is, "Would you be willing to put my birthday in your calendar?" If you are challenged with communicating your needs, or you find yourself in fights that never seem to resolve themselves, I highly recommend you check out NVC courses or books to empower yourself.

The third step to effective communication is actively listening for the needs of the other person. Most people do not listen with the intent to understand – they listen with the intent to reply. If you do not hear or understand what the other person is trying to convey or the needs of the other person, how can you really have an effective conversation with them?

Essentially, active listening involves five stages: receiving, understanding, evaluating, remembering, and responding. As an active listener it is your role to provide feedback on what you hear to the person who is speaking. For example, you might say, "I hear that you feel disappointed that I missed your birthday. To ensure

120

this does not happen again, I will put it in my calendar. You are important to me and I care about your feelings. I'd like to make it up to you in the meantime. I have some ideas, but let's figure this out together." Then offer your ideas for a solution and listen to their input. Initially, if listening is challenging for you, I suggest you practice by taking notes when someone is talking.

Mindfulness Practice & Awarenessing

You are awareness, disguised as a person.
~ Eckhart Tolle

Mindfulness practice occurs when we purposefully and non-judgmentally choose to be fully present with what we are observing, experiencing, or doing, or where we are at any given moment. Through present moment mindfulness, "awareness" gradually arises or is revealed to the mind. *Awareness* is our true nature.

Although we can choose mindfulness in every moment, many people get caught up in a "thinking mind" rather than being present in their experience. They may be stuck in negative memories or future fantasies that cause stress, fear, anxiety and depression due to lifelong habitual obsessive thinking based on confusion from unresolved conflicts that the mind both wants to resolve and tries to prevent. Many habitual thinkers begin to believe they are the "thinking mind" and they get lost in compulsive, obsessive, and negative thinking.

Instead, actively choose to practice mindfulness and cultivate "awarenessing" in your current experience and environment without being caught up in reaction or drama, by simply observing and accepting life, as it is, simultaneously. When we practice present moment mindfulness consistently, we naturally begin to *be* awareness and in that natural state, without the dis-ease of the mind, we experience ongoing, persistent peace, joy and equanimity.

To become more mindful, let yourself be aware of your experience directly, as it is, without commentary from the mind. Simple practices to cultivate mindfulness include meditation, feeling the physical sensations of the body, listening, or watching the breath. Look at the world, without expectation, and see it as it is. Try sitting at a park and simply allow the noticing of all movement or sound. If you go for a run, run without music and listen to your breath or the sounds of nature. Let your senses be heightened by smells, sights, textures, tastes, and sounds that permeate your environment. Young children are amazing mentors to experience present moment mindfulness. Follow their exploration and they will reveal the treasures and pleasures of mindfulness.

Be intentional and clear. When thoughts arise, return to the present moment. If thoughts are particularly sticky, write down what you may need to attend to or resolve, and set a plan to resolve the conflict. If negative judgments bubble up, simply detach and observe them without judgement or attachment, and return again to the present moment.

To get a strong sense of what it is like to experience "awarenessing," when you read this book, read it as though you are watching yourself view the pages and read the words from behind your face or head, like you are looking through the mask of your face.

You can also try watching a movie in a theatre with mindfulness to experience "awarenessing." Let yourself observe everything in the theatre including everyone in front of you watching the film, the sounds, the darkness, the light, the screen and the colors, shapes and movement projected on the film. "Awarenessing" a movie experience this way feels very different than going into the trance of getting lost in the film. Although losing ourselves in a film is part of the experience, testing this out gives us the contrast to see how easily we can get caught in the drama and trance of everyday life rather than being fully present with who we are.

Mindfulness meditations can assist people to feel calm, peaceful and equanimous. They require no religious or spiritual belief to get results. There are various mindfulness meditations available: breath awareness, body scanning, movement, and observing thought.

Responsibility

Most times the mind would like everything to be the way it thinks it should be or that it thinks would make you feel safest. In reality you have no control over how others view the world or how they act. You do, however, have control over how you view, interpret, and respond to events, people, and life itself. Your emotions, beliefs and actions are your responsibility. Let go of any self-imposed expectations or blockages. Who you were in the past is irrelevant to who you **choose** to be today. Choose wisely.

Equality

The Divine entrusts equality to each of us. Establish that all people are your equal no matter where they are on their journey and no matter how their life appears to you. This requires that you accept what the mind might consider the unacceptable: the rejectable, the ugly, the dirty, the crazy, the greedy, or the foolish. Clarify within yourself the truth of equality.

Everyone has come into this existence with a purpose and to learn many things. Every life has meaning. We do not need to do anything or be anything in this lifetime to justify living or being lovable.

From our original Oneness experience, we move into individuated personalities to experience unique circumstances and experiences. Each unique individual expression represents a part of the infinite ocean of possibility of Creation. The Divine allows all.

The moment you judge another for where they are in life, or who they seem to be, you accept and enforce judgment on yourself. You cannot be free of judgment if you judge another. Your mind is listening and watching the rules you create for others and applies them to you too.

Every time you perceive someone as better than you, because you think that they are more talented, successful, or beautiful than you, you establish or reinforce hierarchy rules in your own mind. Comparing and measuring yourself as less than anyone programs your mind to see you as inadequate. The mind then reminds you about what it thinks you want to focus on. For example, if you see another person as being more beautiful than you in a way that makes you feel insecure, your mind will focus on seeing you as unattractive or ugly.

To free yourself from this trap, establish that everyone, including you, is equal. Of course, everyone is unique and individual skills vary from person to person. If someone appears more beautiful, intelligent, or accomplished than you, celebrate their unique gifts joyfully. When you do this your mind orients itself to acceptance and celebration rather than comparison and judgment. To establish yourself as equal to others actively appreciate your beauty and unique gifts too.

When I witness the beauty of another person, I definitely celebrate them in my mind. I will also approach complete strangers to share with them that I see their beauty. Women in particular are deeply touched by another woman celebrating their beauty. When you celebrate the beauty of another you free the mind to focus on beauty rather than on what is wrong with you. I also take time to celebrate my beauty. If I wear something I feel great in, I let myself celebrate. If I complete a project or many tasks during my day, I celebrate these successes too. And sometimes I simply look in the mirror and say, "You are beautiful just as you are."

Men like to be appreciated for their effort, solutions and results. When you compliment a person, it is important to share it from the perspective of how it made you feel. When a woman is told she looks beautiful, she will often deflect the compliment and say something like, "No, I'm not." Although she absolutely wants to be seen as beautiful, she also wants to be seen as humble and a part of her denies her beauty. But the humble act of saying "no" only reinforces to the mind that she is not beautiful and programs her to focus on the negative.

To assist another person to accept a compliment say instead, "Your beauty brings me so much joy." Or to a man you might say, "I really appreciate your help."

Optimalist

Developing the mindset of an optimalist is about learning to fail by accepting that failure is a part of life and a steppingstone to success. As Tal Ben-Shahar describes, "optimalists are not those who believe that everything happens for the best, but those who make the best of things that happen." The key to being an optimalist is being willing to accept reality as it is and then to take action and make the circumstances work for you. It takes courage to accept reality as it is, but the result is a freedom to enjoy the journey of life.[42]

Optimalists also have what Carol Dweck calls a "growth mindset." A *growth mindset* is about orienting yourself to experiment as much as you can in life and learning from failures. The opposite, a *fixed mindset,* is all about I'm either 'good' or 'bad', and if I fail it means 'I'm worthless' or a 'failure.'

With a *growth mindset,* a failure in an area of your life is an opportunity to learn and grow by applying what you learned to be more effective the next time. When things go wrong you might think it is okay, because I can improve.

People who have a *growth mindset* spend their time developing skills and talents. They compare their own growth over time, rather than comparing themselves to others. Conversely, people with *fixed mindsets* judge themselves by thinking their success comes from an innate talent or intelligence; they think their failure confirms that something is wrong with them.[43]

To orient your mind for growth, embrace change and persist when challenges arise. Be patient with yourself and others. We are all just experimenting with life. We are learning what feels and works best for ourselves and our relationships. Orient your goals to reflect improving, progressing, developing, or growing in ways that you would like to experience. Open yourself to learn from the advice, criticism, and the success of others.

Examples

Fixed mindset: "I want to be a loving friend." This statement implies you are not a loving friend. Or it establishes in the mind that you are either a loving friend or not. It is a polarity mindset. Then if you make a mistake, the mind labels you as a bad friend.

Growth mindset: "I choose to learn how to be a more loving friend." This statement implies you are a loving friend who chooses to deepen into friendship. Even if you make a mistake the mind knows you can and are willing to learn and improve, and then the mind orients you to do so.

In conscious friendships this means learning new communication, self-exploration, or leadership skills to help you be a better friend even in the face of relationship challenges. It may also require reorienting your mind for peace if you get lost in anger or rage with another person.

Compassion

No one becomes compassionate unless he suffers.
~ St. Thomas Aquinas

One of the most beautiful states to embody is compassion. Compassion is born out of understanding and love. When you know or can imagine what it is like to suffer, compassion can generate empathy, kindness, generosity, and acceptance. Understanding also happens at a deeper level when we acknowledge that the root of people's suffering or negative behavior is foundational suffering: circumstance (geography or family), poverty (financial, physical, emotional, or spiritual), pain (physical, mental, emotional, or spiritual), stuck mental states, betrayal, and feeling lost, disconnected, alone, or abandoned. When we allow ourselves to feel compassion for others, we get in touch with reality, and we understand better what actions may be required to address the suffering we witness.

At the same time, it is not your responsibility to alleviate the suffering of everyone. There are times when people are placed in your path and you feel moved by compassion to assist them in whatever way possible. Pay attention to the moments when inspiration arises for you, then activate small or significant changes in the field of creation.

When you cannot eliminate suffering for another person, or a group of people, the most important role you play is being a compassionate, unconditional witness to their suffering without letting it destroy you. To do this, hold the other in Truth; beyond their personality and personal experience of suffering they are a powerful, timeless, nameless, and eternal soul. Although difficult and painful their suffering is temporary.

In holding awareness of the Truth of the other, with unconditional love awareness, you impregnate the field and create potential for healing for that person. But more importantly, through you, the other is freed from judgment(s) and any ideas of wrongness. It may be the first gift of unconditional love they have ever experienced. As you love them unconditionally, you offer them the space to be able to remember, reactivate, and restore who they truly are, which is Love, free from the lies they have believed since they first began to suffer.

Love Activism

Those who love peace need to learn to organize themselves as much as those who love war.
~Martin Luther King

Love activism is the active force of compassion. Being a friend to humankind is about stepping up in a leadership role to both embody the traits of a conscious friend and to actively apply the qualities of a conscious friend on all levels of relationships with friends, family, co-workers, clients, community, flora, fauna, and the world.

On an individual level get out, have fun, and get connected. Be an advocate for your own joy, fulfillment, and connection. Get creative, organize social events, and design your own traditions to connect with friends and family in meaningful ways. Establish quality time as a strong value by viewing your personal relationships as a priority in life and setting aside time for friends and loved ones.

Make friends with people who are different from you, whether it is age, race, sexuality, religion, ability, social class, or body size. Disrupt your own biases. You do not know what you do not know.

Be the friend, the help, the support, the mentor, and the leader for those who share your challenges or who you know you can serve. If you feel alone, serve those who feel alone. If you think the world needs to address climate change, find a way to address climate change in your personal life, in your community, or in the greater world. If you fear rejection, then embrace or advocate for those who have been most abandoned.

People of all ages can participate in change. Elders all over the world rise up to protest social and environmental issues. In Vancouver, a group of self-described "sinister seniors" along with hundreds of other protesters were arrested and jailed for their activism against the expansion of an oil pipeline through coastal areas of British Columbia. Across the globe indigenous elders often protest social and environmental atrocities.

Youth activists are also taking a stand for environmental causes and inspiring change in minds worldwide. Dutch environmental activist and innovator Boyan Slat was only 18 when he founded his mission to clean up the world's oceans of 90% of ocean plastic pollution with "The Ocean Cleanup." Greta Thunberg began sitting outside of the Swedish parliament on school days calling for stronger environmental action on global warming with her "School strike for climate" campaign at the age of 15.

At age nine, Canadian environmental activist, Severn Cullis-Suzuki founded the Environmental Children's Organization (ECO) and then went on to address her environmental concerns internationally when she gave her 1992 speech at the Earth Summit in Rio de Janeiro at age 12. Environmentalist Aditya Mukarji started campaigning against plastic straws at age 15.

Let activism begin with love. To bring about environmental, social, and economic change, let love fuel your insight: asking positive solution-oriented questions, using creative imagination and visioning the optimal outcome. Let love fuel your actions for implementing your vision for change: the steps you take and how you take them.

Like you, others are waiting for the world to love and support them. People are looking at the world as a mirror to reflect they are lovable. So, love them. They are you, so love yourself through them. Remind them they are acceptable and lovable just as they are. Remind them they are worthy of care and action-based love. You have a profound opportunity to serve as an evolutionary ambassador of love, friendship, and connection.

There are people throughout the world, even in your community or nation, who are hungry with no one bringing them food. There are children in the world enslaved in sex slavery or in factories with no one rescuing them. There are huge numbers of people in refugee camps with no hope. There are unbelievable atrocities being perpetrated on animals, birds, fish, oceans, forests, and lands across the earth. There are so many people who do not even have access to clean drinking water; they are thirsting for action-based love too.

Recently I sat to meditate with a group of people. I had an unusual experience where I felt extremely cold, beyond what would seem normal. I had brought a blanket and wrapped it around me, but it did not warm me at all. There was a stack of blankets nearby and I asked someone to pass one to me. Again, I was no warmer. One by one blankets were brought to me. I started to cry because somehow I now seemed to feel colder! The cold was so deep and penetrating that it made no sense and I was confused. By the fifth blanket, as it was being placed over me, I began crying with gratitude for the generosity of the woman who brought them to me.

Just after I expressed thank you, God said very clearly, "There are people freezing in the cold and no one is bringing them blankets. There are people who are hungry, and no one is bringing them food." Then very firmly the Divine reprimanded and instructed, "You can do better." Instantly I returned to my normal body temperature and threw off the blankets. Over the course of about 15 minutes, I had been given a very experiential lesson from the Divine in what it feels like to be so cold you cannot warm up and how receiving care warms the heart center and the physical body. I knew God's firm instruction was primarily for humanity the moment it was spoken within me. So be on notice, the Divine is aware that we have the ability and the resources to do a better job at taking care of those who are thirsty, hungry, cold, and enslaved.

Leaders of Influence

Be brave and strategic. Embrace controversy in strategic ways to effect change in the world especially if you are in a role of leadership or influence. Align with the activism of your students, customers, clients, friends and fans. Leaders have a responsibility to speak out and assist others who are disadvantaged especially when the disadvantaged intersect with their business or organization. Create communities to do the work together to lighten the load. Support, inspire, celebrate, and encourage each other.

A community of corporations, called the B Corps, have banded together as a force for good to set standards of excellence to make a positive impact for social and environmental change through business. The B Corps inspirational declaration of interdependence reads:

"We envision a global economy that uses business as a force for good. This economy is comprised of a new type of corporation - the B Corporation - Which is purpose-driven and creates benefit for all stakeholders, not just shareholders.

As B Corporations and leaders of this emerging economy, we believe:

- That we must be the change we seek in the world.
- That all business ought to be conducted as if people and place mattered.
- That, through their products, practices, and profits, businesses should aspire to do no harm and benefit all.

- To do so requires that we act with the understanding that we are each dependent upon another and thus responsible for each other and future generations."[44]

You do not need to belong to a community to set social and environmental standards for your business; you can set your own standards. However, belonging to a community can help to support, encourage and inspire you. What are ways that you can lead and inspire social, economic and environmental change in your area of influence? What are ways that you can lead with compassion in your circle of friends, family and community?

Forgiveness

People stuck in unforgiveness are often tormented by stress, sleeplessness, and obsessive thinking. The roots of unforgiveness are confusion, expectation and lack of understanding. People feel confused when someone they care about betrays their trust or when someone does something that they themselves would not even conceive of doing. They cannot understand why that person would take the actions they have. The mind prefers to know and, if you let it, will not rest until it figures things out.

No one is perfect. People make mistakes of all kinds. You have made a range of mistakes throughout your life too. When you expect that other people should not make mistakes, you program your mind to judge you when you make mistakes. Also, when you expect that other people should not make mistakes, especially ones that directly impact you, you create more suffering for yourself by staying stuck in frustration and expectation. When you accept others as they are, and drop your need for them to be loving, intelligent, harmonious, or whatever else, you free them and you free yourself. Acceptance of others helps create peace within you.

The Divine forgives everything, including your mistakes. The Divine loves and accepts you just as you are.

Orienting your mind to forgiveness is easiest if you are aware that everyone who harms or neglects another has been harmed or neglected as a child and feels disconnected from love and connection. They have been programmed by their own parents and society to believe they are rejectable and unlovable, rather than the Truth that they are Love and are always and forever connected. En masse, most people in the world are lost in the illusion of disconnection and are often triggered by their own fears of rejection.

With your awareness of disconnection in others, be the one who rises above it. Have compassion for those who are suffering in the darkness of aloneness and internal suffering. From this wise state of compassion, understanding frees you from the need to forgive because you recognize the truth that the other is feeling hurt and lost and behaves automatically in ignorance.

But also acknowledge and address the lies you have told yourself about you being unacceptable, rejectable, or unlovable. This frees you to not be so triggered if someone *seems* to reject you or hurt you with their actions. As you reactivate the remembrance of yourself as pure Love, nothing anyone does can hurt you because, firm in Love, you are not pulled back into the illusion of separation. See the *Clarity Process* in Chapter 9 to identify and

135

address the lies you may be telling yourself. If you need help forgiving, use the *Ho'oponopono Prayer* in Chapter 10.

Loyalty & Devotion

One of the blessings of being a devoted and loyal friend is that you provide yourself the gift of developing deep intimacy over the journey of your relationships. Relationships face challenges. That is the reality of interacting with people who are not us. Other people, including our friends, have their preferences, shadow conflicts, and strengths, just like us. We are not always going to agree with or even like our friends all of the time. Giving our friends the safety of not agreeing or letting them take another path is a beautiful gift of acceptance and devotion.

Years ago, due to his wife's jealousy, a friend of mine told me he was breaking up with me as a friend. Instead of making myself or him wrong by feeling rejected, sad, or angry, I felt compassion for his circumstances. I knew he faced a difficult decision.

I shared with him, "We will always be friends even if we never see each other again. You are in my heart and I will always love you and think of you lovingly." I held fast to that choice and awareness. I did not even entertain blaming his wife or making her wrong; she too was suffering. I remained a loving, loyal friend. A few years later my friend contacted me, apologized to me, and asked to be friends again. It was easy for me to transition back to our friendship because I had not allowed his choice, actions, or circumstances or my ego mind to dictate my heart experience of unconditional love.

Brain Wave Coherence

Relationships are able to flourish more when people experience well-being, peace, and ease. Remember to be nurturing, kind, and thoughtful to yourself as you deserve tenderness and compassion. When you are nourished you feel more peaceful and present for yourself and others. Choose to create balance in your life by setting aside time for leisure, exercise, and relaxation. A daily meditation practice is an effective way to increase well-being and peace, reduce stress, anxiety and depression, preserve or enhance cognitive functioning, and improve sleep.

Cultivating deep physiological relaxation and increased brain wave coherence (a peaceful mind), can assist you to be more solution oriented and less reactive in your relationships. Empoweringly, a peaceful state can expand your awareness into deeper states of intelligence, wisdom, and consciousness of who you are, who everyone is and what this life is truly about.

Servant Leadership

The winds of grace are always blowing,
but you have to raise the sail.
~ Sri Ramakrishna

Orienting the mind to be of service through leadership applies many important mindsets, such as equality, compassion, vision, and stewardship. Being of service eliminates the pyramid hierarchy and sets everyone as equals in relation to each other.

To embrace servant leadership, cultivate empathy, foresight, communication skills, self-awareness, receptivity, growth mindset, and contemplation.

Whether you are a friend, parent, teacher, politician, or CEO, you can empower yourself and others to cultivate reciprocal relationships based on respect, meeting needs, and growth as a community. Opening to servant leadership takes the willingness to acknowledge the interconnectedness of us all, to inspire community building, and to assume complete responsibility. At the same time, servant leadership empowers and mentors others to also take responsibility, to participate in decision making and to grow their leadership skills.

A conscious leader invests in personal growth and addresses any emotional conflicts, beliefs, biases, and weaknesses that may block them from serving their community effectively.

A leader in service has deep caring for their community, is committed to the growth of others, fosters well-being, and inspires trust and faith in those they serve. A leader taps into the failures of the past to learn from experience to nurture an advantageous future for the whole group.

A key component of service is assessing the current situation, accepting reality as it is, imagining beneficial possibilities of the future, visualizing a brilliant future, and taking necessary steps to manifest that vision. This can be done in personal relationships as well as in communities, organizations, and companies.

A culture of service inspires loyalty, diversity, productivity, community building, growth, creativity, involvement, team building, and satisfaction in the community.

Gratitude

Gratitude bestows reverence,
allowing us to encounter everyday epiphanies,
those transcendent moments of awe that change forever
how we experience life and the world.
~ John Milton

Experiencing gratitude is attunement to beauty. It is the felt recognition of the beauty of something or someone we perceive. If fortunate, the recognition of beauty is of our own True self. The recognition of gratitude occurs only when one is receptive.

Receptivity, openness, and availability open you to recognize and experience the beauty of life. Internally we may then be able to feel and appreciate the aliveness of life, our health, or positive state of mind. Externally we may be deeply affected when taking in a glorious sunset, connecting with a pet who gazes at us unconditionally, having a prayer answered in a powerful and mysterious way, or recognizing the gift of generosity, kindness, or thoughtfulness from another.

Gratitude opens the heart, balances emotions, eases a worried mind, and rewires the brain. As you practice and then embody gratitude, your mind is opened to beauty and oriented toward appreciation, peace, and joy. Gratitude decreases loneliness, depression, and anxiety.

Gratitude also increases happiness, optimism, life satisfaction, feelings of connection, self-motivation, and resilience.[45] [46] When we feel grateful and optimistic the immune system functions better, but we also take better care of our health and well-being.[47] In addition, people who have started a practice of gratitude have reported that life seems brighter and they have noticed an improvement in their sleep, relaxation, health, and overall well-being.[48]

In the workplace, we find that gratitude and expressed appreciation gives employees a sense of recognition, boosts productivity, releases feel-good neurochemicals, increases intrinsic motivation, and can create an incredible culture of interpersonal connection and optimism.[49] Receiving expressed appreciation is foundational for employees to have a sense of belonging and workplace satisfaction.

Who can you express gratitude to in your workplace? If you lead a team, how can you best express gratitude to your whole team? If you are self-employed, how can you celebrate and express gratitude for your daily accomplishments and successes due to your own actions?

Steps to Activating Gratitude

Can we consciously become more receptive to the beauty of existence and enjoy the nourishing side effects of gratitude? Absolutely! Accessing the beauty of yourself, others, and the world can be cultivated through choosing to be grateful, choosing to participate in or organizing events that put you in the position of being affected by beauty, and having a gratitude practice. Here are some helpful steps to activate gratitude in your life:

1. Actively choosing gratitude is a clear guideline or instruction for your mind. If you find you are in a state that blocks gratitude, such as judgment, envy, anger, frustration, or sadness, use the choice of gratitude to reorient your mind. Say to the mind, *"I choose to feel grateful, to notice and appreciate the beauty of myself, others, nature, and life itself."*

2. Orient yourself to the beauty of life by organizing and participating in activities in nature that move the body in fun and nourishing ways and/or with loving, creative and interesting people.

3. Practice gratitude with your meals. When you sit down to eat, think about all the people who have grown, transported, or prepared that food for you. Think about the technology, finances, businesses, sun, water, soil, plants, animals, bees, microbes that have made that food available for you. Setting up a practice of gratitude, prayer, and blessings for your food before you eat or drink can change the way your body digests your food, as gratitude cultivates relaxation.

4. Implement a daily reflective practice of gratitude by either journaling or sharing with someone at least 3 things you are grateful for at the beginning and end of each day.

What are you most grateful for in your life? Why? How does it bless your life?

Who are you most grateful for? Why? How does that person bless your life?

What is it about you that you are most grateful for? Why? How do you bless your life?

If you want to cultivate ninja gratitude status, find situations, people, and things to appreciate throughout your day. Find people to express your gratitude to. I love writing texts or little notes and leaving them for my friends and family. At least a couple of times a week I phone a friend or family member to express *specific* verbal appreciation.

Every morning for the last ten years I have expressed gratitude to the Divine by saying, "Thank you for this beautiful day!" I have not even lived it; I have not checked the forecast. I assume it will be a beautiful day and it is! Each day is a rich and precious gift from the Divine, with new grace and new opportunities. "*This is the day the Lord has made; we will rejoice and be glad in it.*"[50]

Life can sometimes seem challenging. Keeping a consistent practice of gratitude assists the mind to cope or even feel peaceful by seeing the larger picture of life, rather than getting lost when a challenge arises. You can say: "*Even though I am being challenged in this situation, I am grateful for the blessings of _____.*"

Feeling grateful naturally relaxes you, opens your heart, and helps you feel happier about yourself, your environment, and life. The more you express gratitude the easier it is to embody positivity. When you embody positivity, you change not only your mind, brain, and physiology but magically the field of existence is programmed by your mind. Then life and people begin to respond differently to you. Gratitude opens your heart to others and other people's hearts to you.

Why is it so easy to feel grateful?
Why is it so joyful to appreciate the beauty of life?
Why is it so connecting to feel grateful for my friends and family?

Freedom from Influence

Don't cut the person to fit the cloth.
~Sufi Saying

Many people find themselves pushed and pulled by the needs, emotions, and drama of others. If you are easily influenced by others or struggle to stay in peaceful, clear, loving awareness when interacting with others, there are a few ways to untangle yourself from influence.

- Let others have their point of view. When you find others wrong you lose yourself.
- Let others disagree with your point of view. It is not personal. They have their preferences and reasons. When you allow people to disagree, you choose peace within yourself.
- Let others be reactive to or disappointed in your beliefs and actions. That is their business. In allowing them to have their experience, and you allowing yourself to have your experience, you stay in the power of you. If they express disappointment of you, that is an unconscious projection and has little to nothing to do with you. Let

yourself practice letting others feel disappointed, angry, judgmental, or sad.

- Let go of the need or compulsion to please others. Practice saying, "No," in clear, loving ways.
- Let yourself have your point of view without making others or yourself wrong in anyway.
- Agree to disagree.
- Practice seeing the world differently from others' perspectives. Open yourself to understand why they believe what they do and why they do what they do. Get curious about why someone believes what they believe. Ask them what led them to their point of view.
- Open yourself to unlikely friendships to challenge the familiar influences of your own mind. You never know what you are going to experience, learn, or be blessed by.
- Look for commonalities with other people rather than differences.
- Have fun expressing yourself, supporting others to express themselves, and interacting with mutual freedom. Great friendships have been forged by people with opposing points of view when mutual acceptance is established.
- Stand up for yourself and set boundaries when required. Do this in a clear, non-violent, loving way.
- Remove yourself from situations that are abusive. You never have to stay in a situation that is violent or abusive. Do your best to stay in your power when removing yourself from any drama. Or return to the loving power of you if you have lost yourself in fear, contraction, inferiority, sadness, anger, rage, frustration, shame, or helplessness. Remember, you are Love and return to that.

144

The key to being free of the influence of others is to understand that no one but your own mind is responsible for your anger, frustration, judgment, fear, sadness, being overwhelmed, inferiority, and depleted energy.

To experience your sovereign-self free from the influence of others then you must first choose to free others from your own influence. It is your gift to give first. When you free someone from your influence, you are saying:

- I stop requiring you to be what I want;
- I stop judging you;
- I stop trying to control you;
- I stop trying to make you do something different;
- I stop thinking you should be different;
- I accept you just as you are.

It feels exhausting and depleting to have an opinion about everyone. There is incredible freedom and mental, emotional, and energetic rest in freeing others from your own judgmental influence or controlling beliefs. This begins the process of non-attachment and unconditional acceptance of everyone and everything.

As I mentioned earlier, what you allow in your mind for others, you allow for you. Only when you free the other can you then choose to be free of the influence of others. When you free yourself from the influence of others, you are saying:

- I choose to live as me, just as I am;
- If someone judges me, that is their choice and I choose to accept me as I am;

- I stop trying to control myself to be what other people think is best;
- I stop trying to make myself something other than what I am for someone else;
- I stop thinking I should be different or letting others tell me I should be different;
- I accept me just as I am.

Freedom from Influence Meditation

I first learned about the concept of freedom from influence from a spiritual teacher named Dhyan Vimal. It is a foundational practice that I teach my clients and students and it revolutionized my experience of relationships and life.

Although a simple exercise, it has the power to change your mind, rewire your brain and ultimately transform your life. When you are free of the influence of others you feel peaceful within you. The version I have is similar to his, but with a few changes.

For a minimum of 30 days, preferably 6 months, begin each morning with the following exercise.

For the following exercise you will do a *'Haaaaahhh breath'* between each line by inhaling in through your nose for the count of 7 and then exhaling through the mouth, as you gently begin saying the 'Haaaaahhh' sound at the count of 7.

Sit in a relaxed position in a quiet room with your eyes open but focused on a point across from you in the room. Let your eyes simultaneously take in as much of the room that you can.

1. Declare: I choose to accept the room as it is.
2. Do a 'Haaaaahhh' breath.
3. Declare: I choose to free others from my influence.
4. Do a 'Haaaaahhh' breath.
5. Declare: I choose to be free from the influence of others.
6. Do a 'Haaaaahhh' breath.
7. Declare: I choose to be free from all influences, including my own mind.
8. Do a 'Haaaaahhh' breath.
9. Then sit with eyes open for 5 minutes, seeing the room as it is, and allow any and all thoughts to arise while your awareness is with the sensations of the body, such as feeling your feet on the floor or your hands on your lap.
10. Go into a longer closed eye meditation or begin your day.

Intermittent Freedom from Influence Practice

Throughout the day, if you find yourself reacting to friends, family, coworkers, or strangers, simply declare, "*I choose to free that person from my influence.*" Then, either turn your attention to the beauty of them or turn your mind toward another direction. Notice the green leaves on a tree, the clouds in the sky, or the sensations in your body. You are training the mind to be indifferent to others' actions, beliefs or energies. Simultaneously, you are training yourself to be indifferent to the false, yet familiar, beliefs of your own mind.

Why is it so empowering to free others from my influence?
Why is it so easy to free myself from the influence of the world?
Why is it so peaceful to be free of the influence of my mind?

Chapter 9 - Weeds

*Your task is not to seek for love, but merely to seek and find all
the barriers within yourself that you have built against it.*
~ Rumi

There are malevolent, low vibration weeds that actively choke out
the Flower of Heaven and make it difficult for it to radiate from
your beingness. We know the usual suspects such as envy, jealousy,
frustration, blame, judgment, expectation, and hatred. Additional
weeds include shame, guilt, self-judgment, self-doubt, fear of
rejection, perfectionism, anxiety, beliefs of not being enough and
self-hatred.

Any time you feel the agitation, discomfort, and pain of any weeds
of conflict, it is a clear sign that you are lying to yourself about you.
Once you know that a lie has occurred, it is an opportunity to wake
up from the lie(s) so you can heal into Truth. Anything short of
knowing you are the embodiment of love and connection means
that you are lying to yourself.

Jealousy & Envy

Jealousy and envy are always acts of violence against others, but
also against yourself.

When we feel envious of the beauty, skills, talents, achievements, or opportunities of another, we focus our mind on what we lack. Envy always leaves us feeling miserable, not good enough, rejectable, disconnected, and lonely. When we focus on ourselves as being less than someone else, we live in a prison of fear of rejection.

Whether you fear rejection because you believe you are not good enough, or think there is something wrong with you, or worry that there is something missing within you, you need to address the lack of love and acceptance you have for yourself. Ultimately, you are beautiful, lovable, and acceptable just as you are. I will remind you that your unique beauty and set of skills and interests were purposefully created.

In many cases, to feel better about ourselves, we may try to make the other person wrong or blame them for us feeling not good enough or we may simply project wrongness upon them as a way of not seeing or feeling the wrongness we have allowed within us.

When you make the other person wrong for their perceived and exalted beauty, it is no different to the mind than making someone wrong for their weight, age, or the color of their skin. It is an act of violence to judge successful or attractive people in this way, because everyone deserves respect and acceptance for who they are and the choices they make, the opportunities that bless them, and the work they do to achieve success. No one deserves to be made wrong for being successful, any more than for being stuck. As long as you make anyone wrong for either, you position yourself to receive harsh judgment from your own mind.

It is also an act of violence against you to be jealous or envious because, ultimately, you have made yourself wrong and rejected yourself in comparison to another person. In doing so, you can be triggered by any attractive or successful person. It creates an incredible amount of anxiety in the mind and stress in the body to walk through life constantly being triggered in this way. Furthermore, these triggers can create other behaviors that affect your life in negative ways.

When you make a rule that there is something wrong with another person being successful or having the things you would like to have one day, you program your mind to find wrongness with those successes or states.

- If you judge others for being wealthy, you have instructed your mind that it is unacceptable for you to be wealthy.
- If you are envious of your friend for being married, and let it annoy you or make you feel bad about yourself for not being married, you have informed your mind it is unacceptable for you to get married.
- If you are jealous and angry that someone else at work received a promotion, you are telling your mind to ensure you do not get promoted.

If you would like to be able to see and celebrate your own beauty, celebrate the attractiveness of those you have envied or judged in the past. A loving heart reveals the beauty of existence, including your own beauty.

If you would like to achieve success in an area that requires work, skills, and perseverance, let a successful person be your inspiration.

Remember, although their success may appear to have been rapid and natural, they have most likely spent many years learning, making mistakes, course-correcting, questing, and working to achieve their success. Ask them questions, observe them, learn from the ups and downs of their journey, and celebrate their success.

When you celebrate the success of another, you have instructed your mind that success is valuable, safe, and worthy of attainment. It is also helpful to ask what skills you might need to learn to assist you to achieve the success that would fulfill you. Where would you learn those skills? Who might you ask to mentor you to learn what you need to know? In addition, take note of and celebrate the skills and achievements you have accomplished, so far.

A loving, conscious friend celebrates the gifts, skills, successes, and abundance in the lives of other people. However, it is not always easy to embody automatic celebration of others when you feel insecure, tend to judge yourself, or have low self-esteem. False beliefs about yourself, as well as unresolved emotional conflicts, are always at the root of jealousy, envy, and therefore insecurity, self-rejection, and low self-esteem. These are all great pointers to what needs to be healed deep within.

We are deeply affected by hierarchical programming that is reinforced in the entertainment field, media, and workplace. Jealousy and envy are a result of the pursuit of social status due to the social ranking of society.

We are more susceptible to believing in the ranking system, and striving to be on top, if we learn to believe we are rejectable from our primary caregivers. Parents who are emotionally unavailable, indifferent, uninterested, too busy and/or highly critical set their children up for self-rejection and the need for external validation. Of course, the way our parents are with us is due to the poor mentorship they received from their parents. In addition, if our parents embody shame, we learn and take on the shame of our parents, which compounds the issue.

As we enter the school system, we can then be categorized as good, compliant, helpful and easy or bad, rebellious, troublesome, and difficult. We are consistently ranked in schools based on our grades, social standing, our compliance, and relative beauty.

Movies and TV also actively reinforce "acceptability" memes, as well as the meme of hierarchy itself. In the US, it is challenging to watch a film or TV series about teenagers without the writers creating the same container of characters that have been plaguing and programming Western society since the 1950's. Even cartoons for young children use the same stereotypes and negative social talk that have been passed down for over 60 years.

When we learn to seek validation from our parents and the outside world, it is easy to fall for the idea that if we just fit in, look good enough for others, or achieve great success, all will be right in the world. The pursuit of being *popular, cool,* or *acceptable* is a cult fantasy that many youth surrender themselves to. They are seduced by the idea that if they are accepted by "popular" peers, or by everyone, they will be happy and life will be better. It is a pursuit to be similar to others, to be accepted by others, and for others to determine our worth.

Self-Doubt and Low Self-Esteem

Even the most talented people live their lives and are driven to achieve success or popularity to finally be accepted. They tell themselves the fantasy of:

- If I just do xyz, I'll know I have made it.
- If I make this person laugh, they will accept me.
- If I get good grades, my parents will love me.
- If I get this award, I'll know I will be accepted.
- If I get many fans, I'll know I will be loved.
- If I am a good girl/boy, I will be liked/accepted/loved.
- If I do not ask for anything or need anything, I won't be a burden and I can justify being alive.

Take acclaimed actor Heath Ledger, for example, who at times had crippling self-doubt despite his talent, the respect of his peers, and his huge fan base. Even though Robin Williams was widely adored by fans, created a lifetime of respected work, was deeply loved by friends, and had achieved many awards, he battled with unworthiness and loneliness caused by childhood emotional neglect from absentee parents. He first used humor to get acceptance, love, and attention from his mother. Then he used humor to disarm bullies and to help him feel socially acceptable and liked, as well as to help others feel acceptable. He once said, "I think the saddest people always try their hardest to make people happy, because they know what it's like to feel absolutely worthless, and they don't want anyone else to feel like that."

Artist and inventor Leonardo Da Vinci was known best for his paintings the "Mona Lisa" and the "Last Supper." Few people know that he experienced self-doubt and self-esteem issues. He also had issues with perfectionism which contributed to procrastination and projects left unfinished. Throughout history politicians, inventors, artists, and famous people of all kinds have experienced self-doubt, fears, and low self-esteem.

If you go online, you can search for successful CEOs who share their struggles with self-doubt and fear of failure. Many music artists, especially those with addiction issues, are plagued with self-doubt and fear of not being good enough. Pop artist Justin Bieber shared about his insecurities, bitterness, and jealousy in his letter to his fans after cancelling the last portion of his "Purpose Tour" in 2017.[51]

But what often happens in these circumstances is that people with crippling low self-esteem and self-rejection never feel the satisfaction they are looking for permanently, even if they achieve great success. They may feel it for a moment, or even a day or two. However, when the shine of the moment wears off, they are left with the same unsatisfied mind that makes them wrong again. The underlying emotional conflicts must be resolved in therapy and/or self-inquiry combined with self-acceptance for the mind to feel peaceful and equanimous.

One other option can fast-track you to equanimity: simply choose peace in all circumstances. Assume peace. If your mind makes anyone wrong, including you, then return to peace. Let yourself observe the world with neutral awareness, accepting it as it is. Remember peace.

Self-doubt is natural for most people. Those who choose success in life step forward even in the face of doubt, challenges, criticism, the unknown, and new experiences. They learn what they need to learn to accomplish their goals. They pivot, course-correct, jump over, or duck under obstacles if the way forward is blocked. They take the first step, then the next until they meet their goals.

The fascinating thing is that the *coolest* people are the most comfortable in their skin. They allow their uniqueness to shine through, they pursue their interests, they plan fun activities with their friends, and they do what brings them joy, all from a place of accepting themselves as they are and accepting others as they are.

People who are *cool* rest into who they are. They are not anxious about being accepted. They do not pursue popularity. They have great self-awareness, self-appreciation, self-compassion and take responsibility to move through any self-doubt, insecurity, or negative self-talk. If they ever feel blocked, they hire a coach, talk to a friend, read a book, take a class, go to therapy, listen to a podcast, or just simply take a step even when they feel vulnerable.

True self-esteem is established when we have a personal sense of self-respect. Rather than trying to build your self-esteem through social hierarchy, popularity, or external validation, instead build your self-worth by:

- refraining from seeking validation from others,
- cultivating self-compassion,
- accepting yourself as you are,
- having fun following your interests,

- identifying what skills and goals would be interesting for you to achieve,
- setting a course for learning new skills and achieving your goals,
- being your best cheerleader, and
- celebrating your small daily successes, as well as your large achievements.

Self-compassion allows you to stay in the power of you where you experience inner strength, resourcefulness, and an ability to respond when challenges arise. People who are more self-compassionate are more peaceful and relaxed, have less stress, anxiety and depression, experience a decrease in rumination,[52] and are kinder to others. To develop self-compassion, ask yourself what ways you can comfort, support, accept, mentor, and care for yourself. A journal can be helpful for you to write out your challenges and then ask questions as to how you can resolve those challenges, and to brainstorm solutions or action steps.

Judgment

All judgment is rejection, whether you judge others or yourself, whether a rich person mocks a poor person, or a poor person mocks a rich person, whether a slender person makes fun of a heavy person or a heavy person makes fun of a slender person. And rejection creates a negative state for each person involved, both the victim and the victimizer.

When we judge ourselves or make ourselves wrong or rejectable in relationship to others, we program ourselves for unconscious triggers that may lead to depression, anxiety, hopelessness, or compounding negative thinking. It is challenging when we accept lies about ourselves when we are young, as we often forget what we told ourselves, and then we suffer even more as our reactions, or the lens we view the world through, reinforces our belief and perpetuates suffering. If the lens a person views the world through is dirtied with the mud of rejection, how could they see opportunities for love and friendship? Every interaction, seen through the lens of rejection, would confirm rejection.

For example, during her childhood, one of my clients assumed that she was ugly in relation to her sister, whom everyone complimented from a young age. When she went to college, she observed that was surrounded by beautiful people. She felt defeated and allowed the idea, "Why bother, everyone is more attractive than me." She began to overeat and gain weight. It is wonderful that she could recognize the beauty of others, but unfortunate that because she was programmed by early childhood experiences of believing she was ugly, she used her environment of beautiful people to reinforce the false negative beliefs about her attractiveness, and, until recently, could not recognize her own beauty.

Making others wrong can be a familiar habit that you learned from parents, friends, or even society. You may have had a parent that judged you or was highly critical. If so, you may be so familiar with judgment directed at you during your formative years that you automatically judge yourself. If someone compliments you, you might feel uncomfortable. If someone tries to help you, you might take it as criticism and refuse their help. There are many ways that people embody self-judgment.

If you had a father who judged people based on their economic status, and you chose a career path as an artist or a person who makes a moderate income, you might find yourself severely judging yourself for not being in a position that your father respects. If your parents shamed you around sex, you might judge other people who are sex positive or who easily talk about sex.

For example, a client of mine had an issue with not being able to talk to his partner about sex or to initiate sex. When he was in his early 20's, he recalled going out with his friends, and at the end of the night they would successfully hook up with women. He preferred to feel an emotional connection with and to be in relationship with any woman he would have sex with. Instead of just honoring his preferences, he made his friends wrong for wanting to have casual sex and created an internal judgment about them and other men: "It's not right for men to want to have sex."

He did not know it, but his mind made note of his declaration and made it impossible for him to feel comfortable wanting sex or asking for sex from his partner. To turn it around he would need to do two things. First, accept that it is normal and acceptable for men to want to have sex and to ask for it, even if it is casual sex. I mentioned that his friends most likely went home with women who were looking for the same thing and that those women valued that experience. At the same time, women who value connection would value someone like him. Second, he can reprogram his mind to celebrate men, in general, who want to have sex, whether it is casual or within a monogamous relationship. Celebration needs to be paired with emotional energy, so when you celebrate, get excited, delighted, and enthusiastic! The mind has to believe your declaration. With acceptance and celebration of the other, the mind gets on board for you in the same way too.

Shame

Shame and guilt are two of the most insidious energies that bar you from the Flower of Heaven, as they secretly undermine how you feel about yourself, which radiates out into the world. Some people who carry shame isolate themselves out of fear of rejection. Others who carry shame may be very generous with everyone around them. They may go over and above to be likeable and pleasing to their friends and family. However, they rarely feel comfortable accepting help from others, as they worry about being a burden or being seen as a "taker," which may result in them being rejected.

People can discern when a person gives from the embodiment of strength and wholeness or when they do it to unconsciously manipulate those around them to like them or accept them because they carry shame. Some people feel repulsed by others who, out of fear of rejection, over-give and those who feel repulsed may not understand why they feel discord around such generosity. On the other extreme, some people may use or take advantage of those who carry shame to ensure their personal needs are met without caring about, being aware of, understanding or offering reciprocity.

Those who carry shame are first and foremost programmed to allow others to determine their self-worth. They care deeply what others think about them or what they say, do, or think. This programming most often begins in early childhood with parents who teach us we are unacceptable or rejectable if we behave in certain ways.

Are you hard on yourself? Do you beat yourself up for not being as good as others or for making mistakes?

Do you feel very sensitive to criticism, even constructive criticism, and lose yourself to reactions such as insecurity, self-judgment, embarrassment, and even anger? Do you feel that you are undeserving of love, respect, or success in life? Do you feel as though you must make your friends and family like you by being amenable or by always being helpful and generous? If so, you are carrying shame programming that needs to be healed for you to feel acceptable, lovable, and whole.

To Heal Shame:

To heal shame within you, you need to see others and yourself rightly. This may require deep transformational therapeutic work, such as Rapid Transformational Therapy, Eye Movement Desensitization and Reprocessing, Neuro-Linguistic Programming, or a really talented therapist. I will also add that, 12 Step programs can be helpful for healing shame, as can Christian programs, such as Freedom Session. However, 12 Step programs have their limitations, but as a donation-based program it is sometimes all a person can afford.

Many people do not fully understand shame. They think it is a *thing*. They might say, "I'm shameful," or "My mother was ashamed of me," or "I have shame." If you are one of these people, I'll ask you, where is the shame? Can you see it or touch it? Can you find it if you look for it?

You cannot see, touch or find shame because it does not exist anywhere except as a lie within your mind. The *idea* of shame arises when a person feels less than, unworthy, burdensome, rejectable or that something is wrong with them because someone else or a group of people implied, threatened, or inferred they were not acceptable due to their judgements and expectations. This can happen in person as well as while listening to or viewing media or entertainment. Shame can also happen when someone feels guilty for hurting others or for burdening others.

If you felt shame as a child, see yourself as that child. Look deep into the expectations of another person that shamed you. What was expected of you? How did you feel? What did you believe about yourself when someone placed a judgmental expectation upon you? Would you place that expectation upon a child today? Also, what might have been expected of the person who shamed you when they were a child? Who might have shamed them and taught them that shame was a *thing*? Shame is like a virus that gets passed on from person to person. It only exists because someone taught it to us. Now is the time to retire the shame meme, to uncreate it, and allow loving acceptance to take its place.

Most expectations of children are unrealistic and ridiculous. Children are just learning how to 'be' in this world. To expect them to know what to do, or to expect them do things in a specific way,

162

is a type of insane cruelty inflicted upon the child. It comes from adults who themselves had crazy expectations imposed upon them when they were children. All of this comes from a combination of outdated ancestral and societal 'morals' and beliefs to maintain a rigid system of racism, sexism, classism, nationalism, and ageism, as well as to maintain a corrupted system of disconnection from the Truth of our Divinity.

Permit children to make mistakes and to explore life without criticism. If a child's behavior triggers you, what lies did someone tell you about how to be a child or a human? When my son became a toddler, I remember my automatic response to his exploration was, "No." I had to confront my childhood programming. Why was I so resistant to him getting into things around the house? When we went for a walk, why did I think the path I wanted to take or the duration we spent in one area had to be what I had planned?

I realized my father was very strict about his preferences and there was no room for discussion. It was, as he instructed me many times, "My way or the highway." I learned to be quiet, to do things a specific way, and to anticipate what he would prefer. Essentially, I learned to be co-dependent so that he would not get angry or enraged.

Every time I felt an automatic "No" rise up when my son asked me if we could do something outside of my plans, or outside of what I was taught was acceptable, I replaced it with, "Maybe," or "Absolutely," or "Let me think about that." I began to be discerning, and being flexible became more and more familiar. The gift of my son's intrinsic joy and freedom to explore combined with my willingness to shine the light on the darkness of my upbringing allowed me to release the controlling programs that my father had passed on from previous generations.

Due to my father's anger and clear instructions to not 'talk back' if ever I voiced an opinion, throughout my life, I felt nervous and afraid to ask for my needs to be met or to voice an opinion in groups. I would do it, but my throat would be in a contracted state and I would feel scared. I came off sounding tense or angry; in truth, I was deeply afraid of rejection and being shut down.

The very fear I held inside, and vibrated out to the world energetically, resulted in me being rejected. People could feel something was off with the way I spoke into a space, and felt uncomfortable with my expression, because I was uncomfortable with my expression.

Interestingly, I learned my dad had such fears, as well. He used to get me to make phone calls for him or talk to or negotiate with strangers for him. I wanted my son to be free of the ancestral programming of fear of voicing an opinion or asking for needs to be met. So, I encouraged him to negotiate, explain his point of view, and to try to convince me, if he could. And for my own sanity, I was clear that if I say 'No' or 'Not today' three times, he needs to let it go. He has convinced me more times than not.

Most people who yell at children, or shame them for making a mistake, would never yell at or shame someone at work for making a mistake. As an employee, if you yelled at people at your workplace whenever someone made a mistake, you would most likely be fired. Children deserve respect more, not less than adults because they innocently make mistakes. And yet, so many adults expect children to act as though they are ultra-experienced at life or that they should know better. Even if a child knows better, a child should be spoken to with loving respect to assist them to learn.

When a child believes there is something wrong with them due to criticism, expectations, or judgements, they turn against themselves and experience the ultimate separation. It creates a sense of not being enough, fear of rejection, and self-criticism. To deal with this some children turn on others and begin the process of making others wrong to avoid feeling the depth of their own disconnection. This is also where a feeling of unworthiness or separation from God can occur… if my parents do not value/love/want me, why would God love me?

To begin the process of freeing yourself from shame or any negative emotion, let me help you with a powerful exercise called *The Clarity Process*. It is a gift from the Divine to be used for eliminating any weeds of conflict that may still reside within you.

The Clarity Process

The Opportunity: Every time you find yourself reacting to an event, situation, or person, it is a gateway or an opportunity for you to clear a false belief, which is a lie about yourself. You know you are lying about yourself when you experience any state of contraction: the body feels stressed or you feel sad, angry, frustrated, annoyed, hopeless, agitated, fearful, anxious, or any other negative state.

The way to find the false belief is to follow the emotion. The emotion tells you something is not right. The emotion points to a false belief that you allowed within yourself. It was age appropriate for you to believe the lie because you were inexperienced about the corruption of life. You were also confused as to why others behaved the way they did when they broke your intrinsic Wisdom of love and connection by convincing you of the illusions they believed and learned from their parents and society.

The acceptance of the lie marked your acceptance of programming that has been going on for generations. The false belief is a lie that your mind concocted in response to confusing or traumatic incidents you experienced early in life. To regain your power, it is a blessing to take responsibility for what you accepted as a child. Since you allowed the lie, **you have the power to un-accept the lie** and to free yourself from false beliefs, and to set yourself rightly as the lovable, loving, wise, beautiful, and powerful being that you are.

The mind also tries to hide a lie from you by making you believe that the lie is coming from the other person or that your suffering or your reaction is the other person's fault or that there must be something wrong with you because another person is not being nice to you. But it has little to do with the other person. It has everything to do with a lie you have been believing since you were very little. If you did not believe that lie, another person could say anything mean and you would not believe their statement had anything to do with you being wrong in any way.

Gratitude: Any time you are triggered by someone else's behavior, they are doing you a favor by revealing the lies within you that need to be healed. Practice being grateful to anyone who reveals your unresolved emotional conflicts because now you know where to start your healing.

The Benefits: Each time you wake up to a lie and shine the light of your awareness upon it, you free yourself more and more from the cycle of suffering. You feel lighter, more joyful, free of the influence of others, energized, and your consciousness expands.

When to Use: Use the Clarity Process as soon as possible when emotions and thoughts are fresh.

Steps: Take out a piece of paper and begin answering the following questions:

1. **What happened?** In a clinical way, with just the facts in the past tense, describe what happened without judgment, assumption or what you 'felt' happened. Refer to the other person as "another person" or "the other person." Here is an example of a false statement that is a belief, but it is not a fact: "I felt like the other person hated me." You can describe what you felt as part of the facts as long as your experience is actually a feeling state. You cannot 'feel' that a person hates you. You can feel sad, angry, or frustrated in response to their behavior. For example, you might write, "When the other person said, 'Go away,' I felt sad." Or you can simply write the actions, "The other person said, 'Go away.'" If there is no one else involved and you are aware that you want to heal, for example, shame in general, you would write the belief you have about yourself, as a starting point. For example, "I am not good enough."

2. **What is the emotion?** If you have not written this under the first question, name the emotion(s) that you felt or are currently feeling. No matter what anyone has said or done, each emotion is your responsibility and your opportunity for healing.

3. **What fear is the emotion pointing to?** When did you first experience this before? What was going on in the past that is similar to now? (past experience, internal belief, reactive pattern, etc....)

4. **What is the lie you are telling yourself?** For example, if you feel shame for anything, you need to become clear and ask what is it that I really feel shame for? What is the belief (lie) that I am telling myself about me? Or if you feel sadness ask what is the belief (lie) that I told myself that made me feel sad? The other person could have expressed something mean, but I am inviting you to discover what you believed about yourself when they expressed whatever they did.

5. Go deeper. **What is the lie behind that lie? When did you first experience the lie?**

6. Go even deeper. **What is the lie behind that lie? When did you first experience the lie?** You may even need to go deeper and keep asking until you hit the bottom lie.

7. **Are those lies true?** I can guarantee you that if you blame yourself, feel shame toward yourself, believe that you are not

168

good enough or not worthy of love, or consider yourself rejectable, then you are lying to yourself.

8. **What is true about you?** Hint: You are love, you are doing the best you can, you are enough just as you are, and you are acceptable just as you are. You, just like everyone else, deserves to be accepted and loved because you are acceptable and lovable no matter what you have done or no matter what has been done to you. If I am the only person alive who accepts you unconditionally, then so be it. But I invite you to join me there. I believe that there are other people who love and accept you, too. Maybe their love is conditional in some ways, but not because there is something wrong with you. It is because they have learned to have conditions on love. Let me declare to you right here and now: You are lovable. You are beautiful. You are worthy of existing.

9. **What are some examples of how loving and amazing you are, and were as a child?** If you need to, take out a photo of you as a young child. See how adorable you were. See how much you longed to be appreciated and loved. So, love that young you. Tell yourself, as you gaze at that photo or think of your young self, "I love you and accept you. You deserve love and acceptance and connection. So, I am here for you, always. I am here to be your friend and mentor." Tell yourself all the ways you were and are amazing. Then take that young version of you into your heart centre, so they are always with you: connected.

Blessings in Disguise / Reframing Exercise

Think about an example where you had something traumatic happen in your life and it ended up being a blessing in disguise. I have included a few of my experiences below to give you examples as to how setbacks can be blessings in disguise:

- Feeling deeply alone as a child helped me to open to the Truth of connection so that I may reveal Unity to those who feel separate,
- Having health issues in my late teens resulted in me being deeply educated in health and nutrition for my clients,
- Experiencing intense PTSD and other traumas resulted in me learning how to heal it within my clients,
- Being in a challenging 20-year marriage assisted me to learn how to be free of the influence of another person,
- Getting let go from a job allowed me to step into my life's calling, and
- Missing a flight allowed me to be rebooked to a flight where I was seated beside a woman who became a lovely friend in my life.

One thing I can say with certainty is that everything I have experienced, and everyone I have ever met, has brought me to this moment in my life where I feel the blessing of sharing this book with you. The most traumatic moments in my life have guided me to be able to assist my clients, students, friends, and family to begin to heal and free themselves.

I have grown and flourished despite the emotional conflicts, trauma, programming, depression, anxiety, and roadblocks I faced.

170

I was determined to learn from it all so that I could not only help myself, but assist others to help themselves, too.

Even if you have not been able to recognize the blessings in disguise in your life you can look more closely today. Envision the lotus flower rising up out of the mud to blossom powerfully in the light of the sun. All that dark mud served to strengthen the lotus. So too are you strengthened by the dark mud of your life.

Think about a traumatic event; we could call it the 'poop' of life. Let that manure serve as fertilizer to nourish a deep blossoming within you. Reflect on what has transpired in your life since.

How did the manure of life assist you to blossom?

What blessings came as a result of that difficult experience or situation?

How are you stronger? More skilled? More compassionate? More resourceful?

What did you learn about yourself?

What can you do to continue to heal if more healing is needed? What do you need to learn? Who can you ask for mentorship?

Reclaiming the Garden

Although it is beautiful to experience the Flower of Heaven within your heart center, deepening into loving and conscious friendship is not just about your own personal blossoming. We need to reclaim the garden by mentoring others to experience the Flower of Heaven. As unconditional, conscious friendship blossoms within us, we inform and inspire others to share the beauty of friendship.

Many people did not grow up in families with parents who were compassionate, understanding, emotionally available, and effective communicators. In society, rarely do we see examples of conscious relationships in dynamics between adults and children, amid romantic partners, among policy makers, government officials and its citizens, or in the entertainment industry or in publishing.

We need people to take the lead to co-create a new legacy, new stories of love and respect in our relationships and communities. At the deepest level of our beingness we were born into this world knowing how it should be. We knew that love and connection should be available. It felt confusing and scary when our family and caregivers neglected us or did not know how to meet our needs because they were/are caught up in the illusion of separation, fear of rejection, and the lies of not being good enough within themselves.

Ultimately it leads to great confusion in most babies and toddlers when no one answers their cries at night, when they witness violence or are bullied, assaulted, neglected, or abandoned. In the first few years of life most children blame themselves when others do not meet their physical and/or emotional needs. They cannot conceive that the field of existence is faulty, nor do they consider their parents or friends to be corrupted.

Negative, harmful, and neglectful experiences create self-doubt and self-blame within the child who experiences them. I see these unresolved childhood conflicts time and time again with every client who comes to me for help, whether they are 67, 48, 36, or 12. I have learned how to be an amazing parent from all the neglect my clients experienced that I did not even know was neglect until I saw how their parents' behavior affected them and caused them to be blocked in romantic relationships, friendships, self-esteem, sex, business, career, and finances.

Your parents did the best they could given their programming and circumstances. Most parents thought they were being good parents. They learned from their parents or their grandparents, many of whom were severely traumatized and emotionally disconnected coming out of the devastation of a 1918 influenza pandemic and two world wars.

If you are indigenous, you were most likely affected directly or learned from parents who were severely traumatized by residential schools, kidnapping, the reservation system, and genocide.

If you are African American, you most likely were affected or learned from parents and ancestors who were deeply affected by racism, murder, segregation, abuse, incarceration, degradation, and enslavement.

Whoever you are, whatever traumas your parents or ancestors experienced, somehow that has affected their ability to be emotionally available, which affects your beliefs about yourself.

If you experienced any trauma as a child, first and foremost I personally say: I'm sorry this happened to you. No one had any right to treat you this way. You deserve love, support and acceptance. You deserve success in every area of your life. I love you, unconditionally, no matter what happened to you, no matter what was done to you or not done for you. I also love you unconditionally, no matter what terrible things you have done in this life. And I love your parents and ancestors and accept them unconditionally. My prayer for you and your family is that you all know unconditional love, joy, and peace.

As I have shared before, when parents, family, friends, or teachers behave in hurtful ways it is because they have experienced deep hurt and negative conditioning within them. At the foundation of your True self and their True self, each of you are Love. You are the light the world has been waiting for. Your parents may not have had this opportunity to heal in the way I am inviting you to heal, but you do. Right here. Right now.

You are the blessing your ancestors have been waiting for. You bring in the new energy. It is challenging to be the one who brings the light into the darkness for those who have become accustomed to darkness. They may not know how to receive it or meet you in that place. It may be absolutely foreign to them. Be compassionate and patient with them.

174

If you think that your parents did not meet your needs because they withheld it from you because there was something wrong with you, you are lying to yourself and it is time to wake up from the trance you have been in. It is time to see things rightly to free yourself.

Most parents act in ways that are familiar, the way they were raised and how they were treated. Their unavailability has to do with multiple factors: ancestral and social conditioning, karma (mistakes they have made in this lifetime or past lifetimes), pressures, nutritional deficiencies, emotional disabilities, external circumstances, and being disconnected from themselves.

Be the one to free yourself and to align with love and connection. If you think it should have been so easy for your parents to have met your needs, then meet your own needs and create the life of your dreams. Do what they could not. Be the change you desired throughout your life.

My mother was the last person I loved unconditionally. I had a small amount of expectation that, with a daughter who helped so many people, she should take my advice and improve her life a little bit. I did not have expectation of anyone else, but I expected this of her. My expectation kept me in the darkness whenever I interacted with her. I would become quite agitated and even verbally violent. I could not contain the rage.

At first, I did not understand why I felt so crazy when I spoke with her. So, I did the Clarity Process. I asked myself what the lie was that I was telling myself about her and me. I felt helpless whenever she would tell me all the ways she was suffering. I wanted to help her and was angry with her for not wanting my help. But the biggest lies I told myself was that she should not suffer and that she should improve or at least want to improve her life. My false beliefs caused her to feel judged and me to feel frustrated and helpless. When I realized she has free will to choose her life path, even if that means she suffers, I felt free and peaceful in relationship with her. Now I am free to love and accept her just as she is.

Lies are part of the grand illusion. It is part of what is known as darkness or in some cultures as Maya, Satan, or the devil. Illusion is that which comes between you and Love, between you and your Divinity, between you and God. Anything that takes you out of Love is a lie.

Some people let renovations, death of a loved one, disagreements about money or politics, and so much more come between them and the love they have for each other.

The darkness of illusion creates suffering. Any time you fight with your spouse about money, you are allowing the illusion to come between you and the other.

Any time you reject your parent, you are allowing the illusion to come between you and your parent.

Any time you yell at your child, you are allowing the illusion to come between you and your child.

Any time you see anyone as inferior or superior, you are allowing the illusion to imprison you.

Any time you impose restrictions, expectations and blame upon another person, you allow the illusion to come between you and the other.

Any time you feel shame, allow expectation, or fear rejection, you are allowing the illusion to come between you and the powerful love that you are.

Any time you judge, reject, or shame yourself, you allow the illusion to keep you from love and connection.

Wake the fun up! It is time to remember, reactivate and reinstate our true embodiment of love and connection. It is time to prevent the illusion from coming between us and the love that we are and have for each other. Love is the only thing you can take with you when you die. Love is the only experience of value. Make Love a part of everything you do and allow Love to be who you are.

And in the end, the love you take,
is equal to the love you make.
~ Paul McCartney

Changing Relationship Dynamics

Sometimes being a friend means mastering the art of timing.
There is a time for silence. A time to let go and allow people to
hurl themselves into their own destiny. And a time to prepare
to pick up the pieces when it's all over.
~ Gloria Naylor

There are times we need to permanently shift out of a relationship because we have outgrown a dynamic or we realize we are in an unhealthy relationship or entanglement. At times the dynamic with another person is so strong that we need to take a temporary break to get our bearings or to strengthen our new energy. Other times a friend needs to move on from us.

First, see if you can address your concerns and practice being an unconditional friend even if there are challenges.

If you have to move on or take a break from a relationship, you do not need to make the other person wrong to do so. Some relationships need a little distance from time to time. Not everything needs to be discussed when taking a little time.

If you feel you need to move on from a relationship permanently, talk with your friend first. See if there can be resolution and understanding. If not, let them know what is going on with you. Be honest in a respectful and loving way to allow closure for the other person. This is not always an easy thing to do, but it is an important and compassionate step to take. I see many clients who are blocked in life due to relationships that ended in confusion due to lack of closure.

Even when you move on, keep them in your heart as a friend. If ever you shut down with anger, judgment, fear, reaction, or blame, you are not just closing your heart to them, you are also closing your heart to you. If you are stuck in hurtful emotions, you are most likely lying to yourself about you or them. You may need a little time to see what is really at the root of your strong emotions, but it is important to consciously address the root causes as soon as possible to acknowledge any hurt you feel, see any untruths you are telling yourself, clear all conflicts, and return to the power of Love that you are.

When you move on from a friendship let there be peace and love in your heart. Understand that some people have emotional and social disabilities and limitations. Very few people behave in ways that are purposefully hurtful.

For example, if we take narcissists and avoidant personalities, they are the most emotionally needy people. They are overwhelmed with deep, unconscious, and insatiable needs due to lack of needs being met when they were young children.

Narcissists are often so wrapped up in their needs being met that they cannot even conceive of addressing another's needs, as they do not even perceive the needs of others. It is a very isolating place to live and in order to feel okay they constantly demand that their needs be met.

Avoidants are so unfamiliar with love being available, due to severe emotional abandonment as toddlers, that they will sabotage loving relationships for fear of losing love or feeling uncomfortable in something so unfamiliar. Rather than demonizing narcissists and avoidants, which only keeps you in an unhealthy dynamic with them, you can get educated about the root of their condition and have compassion. Getting educated allows you to also free yourself from their influence in a peaceful way.

Resolution Process

Here is a process that can be helpful to resolve issues when the other person is not present because they have passed away or they refuse to communicate with you. It is called *The Resolution Process*. It came to me as a Divine gift when I was in a state of non-resolution with another person. At the time, I was in great suffering. I sat down and questions came into my conscious awareness one after the other as I answered each question.

Every conflict is a clue and an opportunity to heal our deep wounds. Our closest relationships reveal what is most unhealed within ourselves. Self-awareness and presence are key to healing yourself, creating a safe place for all parties, and deepening into intimacy with the other.

Almost everyone has unresolved emotional conflicts, so you are in similar company.

Some people avoid romantic relationships as they search for the "perfect" partner. Others make their current partner wrong to justify leaving them. Some people avoid social relationships altogether. Far too often I hear people say they would rather watch something online than hang out with people. Lovingly, resolve your issues. We are called to heal what is within us to learn, grow, explore, and deepen into loving connection.

Observe what triggers you and how you react. What are the lies that you tell yourself about <u>you</u> when someone behaves in a hurtful way?

Resolution Process Instructions

If you have an unresolved conflict with someone who is alive or has passed away and you are ready to resolve the situation without them, then take out a notebook or a piece of paper to write down your answers to the following questions:

1. **What is the end goal?**

   This really comes down to the ideal state of mind, embodiment or situation for the relationship or for this situation or for yourself. For example: peace, love, truth, freedom, etc. What do you want to see happen within you or your actions? Write down that simple word or two in capital letters. For example: PEACE Once you write it down, tell yourself: "I choose peace. It's empowering to experience peace." When you are doing this process, always keep your end goal in mind.

2. **What happened?**

   Just the facts, Jack! In a clinical way, with just the facts in the past tense, describe what happened without judgment or assumption, and without belief of what you "felt" happened. Refer to the other person as "another person" or "the other person." You can describe what you felt as part of the facts as long as it is your experience of feeling. For example: "When the other person told me, 'You didn't do a good enough job,' I felt embarrassed." Here is a statement that is a belief but is not a fact: "The other person thinks I'm incapable."

3. **What can I learn from this experience (about me)?**
Automatic reactions are always based on subconscious beliefs. When we name them, they become conscious and we can state them in the past tense. What were your subconscious and automatic reactions? In what ways were you lost? For example:
a. I had a subconscious and automatic reaction to another person's apparent rejection of me.
b. I had a subconscious and automatic reaction to another person's anger, frustration, fear, or sadness.
c. I was lost in a fear of rejection mindset.
d. I was lost in feeling anger that another person didn't _____.
e. I was lost in feeling frustration that another person wasn't willing to _____.
f. I experienced a similar situation a few years ago, when I was young, or the other day.

4. **What situations trigger me to react? Has this situation come up before?** Describe the pattern.

5. **What is my responsibility to shift?** What illusions/lies did I believe and need to shift? What frequencies are my responsibility to heal? For example: It's my responsibility to:
a. Heal any frequencies of fear of rejection.
b. Heal any frequencies of fear of loss of power.
c. Heal any beliefs where I believe another person has to listen to me or has to want to listen to me.

d. Dissolve any illusions around me not being good enough.

e. Free other people from my influence and free myself from any influence.

f. Reprogram my subconscious to allow another person to be as they are without it influencing my embodiment.

g. Refrain from rejecting me and then rejecting the other person.

h. _____ me. I choose to _____ me. (love, respect, honor, celebrate…)

6. **What is the vision you hold for your embodiment?**

   What are you embodying in your future vision? For example:

   - I am embodying…. or I am enjoying…. or I am joyfully….)

   - I am embodying peace and love.

   - I am enjoying the freedom to be me just as I am.

   - I am joyfully accepting myself just as I am.

7. **Afformations**

   Many people are familiar with *affirmations*, which are positive statements made to convince the mind of something else you would like to embody. An example would be, "I am beautiful." *Afformations*, on the other hand, are powerful questions. An example would be, "Why is it so joyful to feel beautiful?" These questions are not for your conscious mind to figure out. The questions are posed to the subconscious mind to prompt it to look for the answer. In the process of looking for the answer, the mind attracts the state and circumstances it is focused on.

Come up with at least five afformations to reprogram your subconscious beliefs. Use your *vision statements* from step 6 and any old patterns to come up with potent questions. Ask these questions at least once a day for 21 days, as you feel the joyful states you are describing. For example:

a. Why is it so easy to embody peace and love?
b. Why is it so peaceful to be present?
c. Why is it so joyful to love me?
d. Why is it so freeing to love others?
e. Why is it so peaceful to relax?
f. Why is it so joyful to embody love and celebration?

8) What did I learn about myself from this exercise?

Chapter 10
Forgiveness & Reconciliation

Forgiveness is the fragrance that the violet sheds
on the heel that has crushed it.
~ Mark Twain

When you heal, you forget the suffering you lived with and you are free of the illusion.

Even though you desire joy and peace and self-acceptance, you are the one who keeps you from it. No one else. You have kept yourself in a prison of blame, shame, and you have been critical of yourself for much too long.

Return to the remembrance of the beauty of you. It is that simple. Let go of the coat of shame. Choose right here and now to honor yourself, to love yourself, and to nurture yourself. Let it be your remembrance of your most Holy self.

You, my dear, are a child of God. Let you honor the creation that you are, equally to the beauty of a sunset or a newborn baby or a beautiful vista. You are glorious. And if no one shared this with you before, here I AM declaring your beauty.

I invite you to remember, to choose the remembrance of the beauty of you. No one can reveal this to you. Only you can choose this for you.

If you have hurt others, ask for forgiveness and move into the beauty of you. If you have hurt yourself, ask for forgiveness.

Let your remembrance guide you out of the disconnection. When you allow the beauty of you, go into the world and allow the beauty of others.

Ask God to forgive you and forgive yourself for any self judgement and lack of responsibility.

Say to God and yourself,

- *Forgive me for being unkind to myself and others.*
- *Forgive me for neglecting care of myself.*
- *Forgive me for dishonoring myself.*
- *Forgive me for not always choosing the optimal and most nourishing path for myself.*
- *Forgive me for not being present with my child, family or friends.*
- *Forgive me for feeling not good enough about myself.*
- *Forgive me for being afraid of failure or success.*
- *Forgive me for being afraid of rejection.*
- *Forgive me for the simple and the complex ways I have made mistakes.*
- *Forgive me for judging my appearance.*
- *Forgive me for comparing myself.*

- *Forgive me for all the ways I withheld love from myself or others.*

- *Forgive me for the lies I have told myself.*

- *Forgive me for the ways I mistreated Love.*

- *Forgive me for the people I shunned, belittled, rejected, and judged.*

- *Forgive me for being distracted from Love.*

- *Forgive me for rejecting Love.*

- *Forgive me for forgetting my own beauty and the beauty of my family and friends.*

- *Forgive me for wishing I was someone other than I am.*

- *Forgive me for hiding myself and covering the inner beauty of me.*

- *Forgive me for the battles I have fought and maintained with others.*

- *Forgive me for forgetting to rest, play, and laugh.*

- *Forgive me for forgetting the beauty of creation.*

- *Forgive me for getting lost in unhealthy dynamics or self-destructive behaviors.*

- *Forgive me for rejecting my mother or father in any way.*

- *Forgive me for allowing myself to believe I am unacceptable because my parents were not able to mentor me because they were stuck in the illusion.*

- *Forgive me for getting lost in the illusion.*

Go forward and treat every person as the equal child of the Divine that they are, no matter how much they have forgotten their beauty, no matter how lost they seem.

Love them unconditionally.

Let your Love for yourself and for your brothers and sisters of the world redeem all past transgressions.

Ask the Divine to guide you and instruct you in what Love would do in all circumstances. If you go into any negativity, ask for Loving Mentorship. Choose peace. Invoke the peace of Love.

If you are being called to take action, let it always be with peace in your heart and clarity in your mind. Take responsibility wherever you have the means to do so for your actions or non-actions.

Dear God, I pray that the beauty of me is revealed to me, not just for me, but so that the remembrance of me allows me to remind my friends, family, and my brothers and sisters around the world.

Remember me to you, dear Loving God.
Remember me to me.
Remember me to the beauty of creation.
Remember me to how I may live in peace, love, and harmony.
Remember me to respect all sentient beings.

Remember me to respect the Holy earth, the beautiful home you created for <u>all</u> of us.

Remember me to lovingly support all those who protect our home, who work for the equal rights of everyone, and who feed and care for the poor in my community and beyond.

God entrusts each of us to ensure equality.

God is THE author of Love. If you want to love yourself, or your brothers and sisters, go to the Master of Love and request that you be mentored. You can also request mentorship from God's entrusted Holy beings that are there specifically to serve you and mentor you, like Christ or any Buddha of Compassion and Love.

Ask Peace to mentor you in peace.

Ask Love to mentor you in love.

Ask Wisdom to mentor you in wisdom.

I am here to remind you that beautiful Divine mentorship is available to you. God created you and knows you intimately. God awaits your remembrance of the Everlasting Unconditional Love that is God.

If you are caught up in unforgiveness, God cannot intervene, due to free will. If you want forgiveness to be in your heart, you need to choose forgiveness before God can grant it.

If you are harboring ill will or emotional conflicts with anyone and you want resolution from this point on, hear this: God entrusts you to choose forgiveness both for you and the other person.

If you believe someone harmed you, or if you have been harmed and you are suffering, this message can be the life-raft to brings you to the shore of peace, love, and harmony within you.

If someone is mean or neglectful in anyway, including your parents, it is because they are lost. If you stay in unforgiveness, you have joined them and are lost with them in illusion. If you want to get out of that lost state, choose to remember your Divinity. You, my beautiful, are Love and you are loved.

No matter what people say about you or the way they treat you, remember Love. Activate, in that moment, the power of Love. Stay in the power of Love. BE the remembrance of Love.

If you ever lose yourself, re-read the previous paragraphs. If you falter in anyway, humbly ask God for forgiveness and to heal any blockages to Love and get back to Loving yourself and the world.

Every day, every moment, renew yourself in your choice. Keep it simple. Let yourself be mentored by one mentor. It could be Love, it could be Peace.

God invites us to return to mentorship. In many ways it is the allowing of yourself to be like you are a kindergarten student, but it is not like any kindergarten you have ever known or experienced before. When you surrender to the mentorship of the Divine, you enter into states of peace, love, and wisdom.

If ever you suffer, you have stepped away from Divine mentorship. It is your choice to return again. You are always welcomed into the mentorship of God.

You may want God to rescue you from your suffering. Certainly, the Divine is there blessing you with help whether you recognize that help or not. At the same time, you will not leave suffering unless you first choose to acknowledge the invitation to remember your Divinity. Of course, you can simply choose to acknowledge your Divinity. You have been sleeping in the nightmare of illusion. I am waking you by reminding you…

Stay in the Power of You

In any given moment, you can be in the power of you simply by being present in this moment without the fantasies of the past or the future. If someone is mean to you, you lose yourself when you allow a thought that you are being hurt or there is something wrong with you. Simply stay with the present moment fact: that person is expressing anger at you or toward you. Stop making it about you. Let it be about their experience. You do not have to join them there, nor do you have to conjure up a negative fantasy about you. You do not have to reject them, nor do you have to reject yourself. You can simply be an unconditional witness to their action.

Stay in the power of you by surrendering your will to God and aligning with God.

I choose direct mentorship with you, God.
I choose to be mentored in Love by God.
I choose to be remembered into Divinity.
I choose to keep my focus on my Divinity.

191

I am a child of God, this body, mind and soul are surrendered to God, my existence is sealed in God. Coming home to the present moment awareness of me right here and now.

I choose to be here, now, in Truth, Love and Peace.

If you get pulled into anything negative or obsessive, keep coming home to you, until you are firmly in the power of you embodying peace, love, and harmony.

Ho'oponopono

Ho'oponopono is a beautiful and transformational practice of forgiveness shared from the ancient Ho'omana tradition, also known presently as the Huna tradition of Hawai'i. Ho'omana teachings arrived in Hawai'i sometime between 750 and 1250 AD, and their origin is unknown.

Ho'oponopono is a combination of words that mean *to make right, to put in order*, or *to correct*. It is a practice that allows one to correct or amend the wrongs or the misguided actions that one may have made in relation to another. Forgiveness is a very powerful tool that can be used to clear your karma as well as the karma of others.

Essentially, the first stage of forgiveness is taking responsibility for what you are consciously aware of, and whatever else you might possibly be responsible for doing. The deeper level of forgiveness comes from the compassionate understanding of karma and our interconnectedness with people who have caused us harm. As a person harms me, I have most likely caused them harm or someone else harm in this or a past life. To break free of the pattern of suffering, me forgiving them and asking for forgiveness allows for both of us to be free.

An even deeper wisdom of forgiveness is the understanding that we are 'all one.' At the most basic level, if someone in my community was robbed by another person in my community, I am responsible for that suffering. As a community, the perpetrator suffered in a way that created circumstances for him to steal from another. Maybe 'we' allowed a system to occur that did not provide adequate support for his parents. At the most profound level of oneness, I am the social worker who did not do their job to ensure this young man's family had what they needed. Or I might be the person who knew his parents needed a job because they were out of work for six months but did not try to help them. Or I am the father of this young man, and I refused to work.

Ho'oponopono is based on the principle of 100% responsibility, which means taking responsibility for everyone's actions, not only for your own. You are at the center of your universe. It is your experience.

"If one would take complete responsibility for one's life, then everything one sees, hears, tastes, touches, or in any way experiences would be one's responsibility because it is in one's life. The problem would not be with our external reality, it would be with ourselves. To change our reality, we would have to change ourselves." ~ Dr. Hew Len

If 100% responsibility is a big leap for you to consider, then begin with what you know you are absolutely responsible for, and also what you may be responsible for. If you tend to be critical of others, have a habit of blaming others for their circumstances, or are highly critical of yourself, Ho'oponopono can be a beautiful blessing of transformation.

I first heard of Ho'oponopono through an interview I watched with Dr. Hew Len, who learned of the practice through Morrnah Simeona. He developed and taught an abridged version of Ho'oponopono to the general public, which is very different from Morrnah's version.

I developed my version below based on Dr. Hew Len's. But I was Divinely guided to expand it and to include a specific breath with the prayer. It is only recently that I learned of Morrnah's original version, which has some similar aspects to mine. Morrnah's original Ho'oponopono prayer is a 12-step process. I recommend that you look online for the version by Morrnah Simeona and try both hers and the one I have included below to see which works best for you.

Ho'oponopono Prayer

As a powerful practice of clearing unresolved conflicts (karma) between you and others, as well as healing your inner conflicts, I recommend using the following forgiveness prayer for all your relationships present and past. As a daily practice do Ho'oponopono for one person before you go to sleep each night for a minimum of 30 days to 6 months. The people you do this for can be anyone you have a conflict with or have harmed, but it can also be done for your loved ones and friends.

To use Ho'oponopono to resolve specific conflicts between you and someone you know, follow the steps below.

First Night, Clear You to You

The first time you do Ho'oponopono, begin by doing the practice below for yourself and all beings. Ask forgiveness from yourself for any and all harm you have caused your personality, your mind, and your body.

Then address the Divine and ask for forgiveness for any and all suffering you have caused anyone in this lifetime or any other lifetime. Ask the Divine to guide you into healing all the places where you have not yet forgiven others. Ask the Love and Wisdom of the Divine to bless your mind, body, and soul in all ways. Ask the Divine to forgive anyone for any and all suffering they have caused you in this lifetime or any other lifetime.

Next Steps

Once you've completed the first session for yourself, begin with the people closest to you, including any current children or a child to be. Then bless anyone with whom you have issues or conflicts. Next, address your extended family and even your ancestors. Of course, if anyone comes up in your mind from any time in your life, you can also do forgiveness practices for yourself and them. Feel free to include pets or animals you may have harmed.

The first part of this prayer is based on Dr. Hew Len's version of Ho'oponopono. I received Divine inspiration for the additional three parts in order to complete the clearing.

Begin by bringing the person you would like to forgive to your mind. Call infinite Divine Love into your heart center and imagine your heart center as the gateway for Divine Love to radiate out from. It radiates to all aspects of your being and fills up your body and energy field. See a beam of connection from your heart center to their heart center. If you have difficulty imagining this, just tell yourself that you choose to connect in this way, and assume the connection is established. When you ask for forgiveness, it includes the actions you did not know caused harm or that were accidental.

Then say, "Dear person's name. I love you. I am sorry for any and all suffering that I have caused you in this lifetime or any other lifetime. Please forgive me. Thank you. Thank you. Thank you."

Then do a 'Haaaaahhh breath' by inhaling in through your nose to the count of 7 and exhaling through the mouth as you gently begin saying and extending a 'Haaaaahhh' sound to the count of 7.

Now move on to the next 3 parts of the prayer below.

Summary of Ho'oponopono Prayer

Dear _____.
I love you.
I am sorry for _____. I am sorry for any harm I have caused you in this lifetime or any other lifetime.
Please forgive me.
Thank you. Thank you. Thank you.

(Haaaaahhh breath)

Then address that same person and say:

Dear _____
I love you.
I choose to forgive you for any harm you may have caused me in this lifetime or any other lifetime. I forgive you and I forgive any debts you may owe me.
May you know peace and love.
Thank you. Thank you. Thank you.

(Haaaaahhh breath)

Then address God and say:

Dear God,
I love you.
I am sorry for any harm I have caused _____ in this lifetime or any other lifetime. Please forgive me.
Thank you. Thank you. Thank you.

(Haaaaahhh breath)

Then address God regarding the person who has harmed you and say:

Dear God,
I love you.
I forgive _____ for any harm s/he/they may have caused me in this lifetime or any other lifetime.
Please forgive them/him/her. Forgive all debts that _____ may

197

owe me.

Bless them, send them the light and love s/he/they needs to heal and know peace.

Thank you. Thank you. Thank you.

(Haaaaahhh breath)

My Prayer for Us

Here is a prayer that I share, right here and now, for you and me:

Dear Divine Soul of you who are reading this, everyone in existence, nature, and all of creation,

I love you. I humbly ask for your forgiveness for any and all suffering I have caused you in this lifetime or any other lifetime, directly or indirectly, due to my lack of awareness of my Divinity. Forgive me for not feeding you when you were hungry. Forgive me for attacking you or enslaving you. Forgive me for forgetting you and for forgetting myself. Forgive me for polluting you or corrupting you. Forgive me for rejecting you and neglecting you. Forgive me for fearing you or scaring you. Forgive me for teaching disconnection and suffering. Forgive my confusion and lostness.

Please forgive me.

I choose to forgive you for any suffering you have caused me. I forgive any debt that you may owe me due to you not knowing your Divinity in this lifetime or any other lifetime.

May you know the Truth of the Holy Love of God.
May you reside in Peace, Love, and Harmony.
May the Grace of the Holy Mother nurture and awaken you.
May the reconciliation and remembrance of your Divinity bless the world.

May the Grace of your Holiness be upon you.
Thank you, thank you, thank you.

Dear Divine Soul of the Merciful Highest Creator,

I love you.

Dear God, please forgive me for any and all suffering I have caused myself or others in this lifetime or any other lifetime. Forgive me to you. Remember me to you always. I surrender to your will, mentorship, and blessings.

Dear God, please forgive my sisters and brothers for any and all suffering they have caused me in this lifetime or any other lifetime. Forgive any debt they may owe me. Free them to know peace, love, and harmony.

Thank you, thank you, thank you.

Love, Tara

Additional Healing

We create beneficial cords of connection for those with whom we do this practice. If you feel for any reason that there are non-beneficial cords, you can consciously choose to uncreate those non-beneficial cords. Ask to be shown those cords that no longer serve you and the other person. You can imagine them in your hand and pray:

"In the name of the Highest God (Creator of All, Allah, Christ, the Divine, etc.) I pray this (these) cord(s) be dissolved."

Imagine them dissolving immediately and completely. Say out loud, *"They are gone, done, destroyed. I am free to be me, just as I am. I am free to love the world, just as I am."*

You have completed the forgiveness prayer for someone when you can think of that person without any negative emotions or contraction in your physical body. For some people you may need to repeat the forgiveness prayer another time, as the relationship may require further acknowledgement or learning of some kind.

Why is it so freeing to forgive?
Why is it so joyful to lovingly accept others as they are?

Chapter 11
Prayers of Friendship

Prayer does not change God,
but it changes him who prays.
~ Soren Kierkegaard

Prayer is both a powerful tool for change and an intimate communication with the Divine. You can pray anywhere or anyhow. You can sing, speak, dance, paint, or cook your prayers. As love activists, we can let our actions sing our prayers. We can pray to request assistance for another, or to ask God for Grace for ourselves.

Powerfully, we can also use prayer to express gratitude to the Creator for the blessings in our life, or even to maintain an intimate relationship with the Divine. Think about how many times you text a friend. If you send a heart emoji to God as many times as you text everyone else, your connection with the Divine might be very different than it has been.

As we deepen in prayer, as a form of surrender meditation, we can enter into communion with the Divine.

If you feel curious or called to connect with yourself, others, or the Divine in deep and powerful ways but you feel stuck, blocked, or not sure how to really get there, then prayer can be a wonderful tool to connect.

Can prayer change things?

Yes and no. We need to account for many circumstances when we pray. Prayer can change things, though we may not see the result. It is best for prayer to be offered without expectation, but expectantly and hopefully. For example, if someone is dying and we pray fervently for their healing, our prayer may or may not be answered. We need to consider the path and the will of the person dying. Everyone is born into this existence at a specific time, not one nano-second before or after. With death everyone experiences a very precise time for their departure too.

Why pray then?

Think of prayer as a dance, in which we are called to participate, as one of the many experiences we share with others. It is an honor to be moved in loving compassion to pray for the best outcome for a loved one or a group of people, in a time of challenge or transition. The depth of our love for them, our concern, and care is a blessing for them, for us, and for the world. When we are brought to our knees, humbly not knowing how to be or what to do, we surrender the ego. The mind cannot figure it out. The heart calls out! Pain and anguish happen because we are in conflict between what is and what the mind thinks should be.

When our prayers are not answered in the way we had hoped, we can learn patience, acceptance, curiosity, and openness to a greater mystery that may not be understandable to us… at this time. When you pray allow yourself to be moved with heartfelt compassion and at the same time surrender to the will of the Divine's plan.

Powerful Keys to Prayer

God speaks in the silence of the heart.
Listening is the beginning of prayer.
~ Mother Teresa

Throughout my life being Divinely inspired, reading many sacred texts, and learning from experience and generous spiritual teachers has guided me to have a deep sense of what contributes to powerful and effective prayer.

Gratitude - Begin each prayer with gratitude. Establish your recognition that in many ways you are blessed. What blessings can you acknowledge? I like to begin with, *"Dear Highest God, I love you. Thank you for your blessings today both seen and unseen, known, and unknown."* Then I will recall and recount a few of the brightest blessings I have noticed that day or week.

Connection - When you approach the Divine, set an intention of connection. Open your prayer like you would start a letter or a conversation with a friend: "Dear Divine," "Dear God," or "Hello, dear Creator, I love you." What is the most comfortable way for you to start?

Then visualize yourself connecting with the Divine; envision a connection between your heart and the heart of the Divine, however you can imagine. Or see yourself in the heart of existence. Or tell yourself and feel the following: *The Divine loves me.* Use your imagination to be clear that you intend to connect. The more you imagine and feel, the more powerful the experience.

Curiosity - Get curious about everything you would like to shift, heal, change, or know. Asking questions in prayer is a powerful way to receive mentorship from the Divine. Ask God, *"How do I learn to hear your guidance? What do I need to know to heal the suffering I am experiencing? How do I open my heart to my neighbor or colleague? Who do I need to meet to get that project done?"*

Listening & Discernment - As you draw near the Divine in your prayers, listen for guidance and direction. Take time in stillness and silence to allow God to guide you. The art of prayer requires you to cultivate receptivity and listening attention in relationship with the Creator. These are also important skills to nurture in your friendships with others. As you strengthen your listening skills with people, you learn to attune with God. As you attune with God, you attune with others.

Humility and Worthiness - It is important to approach the Divine with humility. If you recognize the Divine as wiser than you, and that you are being mentored or guided by the Grand Orchestrator, you empty your need to be right or to think you know the best way. This humility is a fine line. At times we may not feel worthy of the Grace or forgiveness of the Divine, because of something we have done. Let go of unworthiness. It is not a healthy place to stay. You, like everyone else, are worthy of Divine blessings.

Remember, you are the Sacred Creation of the Sacred Creator; you are a Divine Child of God. You were born in love, out of love, intended for love, and are therefore worthy of love, connection, forgiveness, and Grace with the Unconditional Lover of us all. Most of my prayers at home often start on my knees with my forehead to the floor. By the end, I am either upright on my knees or standing with my arms reaching to the sky in a position of receptivity.

If I am out in public, I will place my hands together in prayer position and imagine myself bowing to the Divine. Even if others are around, I am not shy to raise my hands up in celebration and receptivity.

Sincerity - The most foundational element to praying is sincerity. Let your heart align you with what you are trying to share with, or ask from, the Divine. Share what you are feeling and what you are believing, even if it may not be true. What I mean is, if you think there is something wrong with you or a situation, it does not mean that it is true. Be as clear as you can be. You may not have the words or ability to even think them, but the Creator knows your heart and mind. The Divine will hear your prayer.

Just put it all out there with God. If you feel sad, angry or frustrated, lead with that. Share with the Divine, "I am feeling sad because _____." Or reveal, "I feel this sadness in my heart or in my abdomen or throat."

Faith & Surrender - Enter into the sacred field of faith, faith in a higher power, a savvy Creator of everything. Trust in the greater Wisdom of God. When you pray, surrender to the will of the Creator of All by acknowledging after your request that the highest good and greatest joy of the individual, yourself, and the world be done, by the Wisdom and Will of God. When needed, I pray,

"Dear Divine, I pray for Wisdom and Understanding. What is it that I need to know about this issue so that I may take responsibility and heal what is unresolved? May you bless me with your Wisdom and Grace. Whatever blessings I receive I will use them to help others. Thank you, thank you, thank you."

People may ask, "Should I just blindly believe in God or a higher power?" I am not sure it is blind. There are about 10 billion galaxies in the observable universe! The body itself is miraculously made. The body has anywhere from an estimated 30 to 100 trillion cells. It is self-healing and operates without your influence for the most part. You do not have to digest your food, your body does it for you. You do not have to detox your brain, your body does it for you every night when you sleep.

You are just one organism among billions of the human species. To date, there are over 1.3 million species that have been identified and most species have not yet been identified. In addition, there are over 75 billion tons of living things on Earth. The interconnection of species is profound, from the orchid bees that pollinate the Brazil nut tree to the protective ant species that herd aphids in order to have a constant supply of honeydew that the aphids produce. Species have been coded to interact and rely on each other. I am in awe of the whole system.

God writes the Gospel not in the Bible alone,
but also on trees, and in the flowers and clouds and stars.
~ Martin Luther

Blessings & Conscious Maximum Benefit - Ask that your prayer be not just for your benefit but also for the benefit of everyone involved and for the world. For example, let's say someone is going through a breakup. They may <u>want</u> to stay with their partner, but they may <u>need</u> to move on. For them to pray for reconciliation may not be for their benefit, nor the benefit of the other person.

A more conscious prayer might be: Dear Divine, I love you. I'm feeling so sad that my partner broke up with me. I don't know what to do. Forgive me* for any and all mistakes I have made with my partner or with myself while being in relationship with them. Let your Grace bring wisdom to this situation. Let me see the blessings of our time together and let me know the blessings of us separating. If we are meant to be together, bless both of us to heal whatever needs to be healed within us. If we are not meant to be together, bless both of our paths with Love, Wisdom and Grace. May we know peace, joy and love. All this or something better. Your will be done, dear Wisest One. Thank you, thank you, thank you.

*Asking for forgiveness is not about placing blame with yourself. It is about taking responsibility for anything you may have done that has contributed to the situation.

Gratitude - End your prayer with gratitude. Express gratitude as though your prayer has been answered. Feel the gratitude in your heart center.

Powerful Prayers to Connect with the Divine

O Allah, allow me to love You and to love those who love You, and to love whatsoever brings me nearer to Your love, and make Your love more precious to me than cold water to the thirsty.
~ At-Tirmithi

Prayer of Peace

Lord, make me an instrument of your peace:
where there is hatred, let me sow love;
where there is injury, pardon;
where there is doubt, faith;
where there is despair, hope;
where there is darkness, light;
where there is sadness, joy.

O divine Master, grant that I may not so much seek
to be consoled as to console,
to be understood as to understand,
to be loved as to love.
For it is in giving that we receive,
it is in pardoning that we are pardoned,
and it is in dying that we are born to eternal life.
Amen.

Serenity Prayer by Reinhold Niebuhr

God, give me grace to accept with serenity
the things that cannot be changed,
Courage to change the things
which should be changed,
and the Wisdom to distinguish
the one from the other.

Living one day at a time,
Enjoying one moment at a time,
Accepting hardship as a pathway to peace,
Taking, as Jesus did,
This sinful world as it is,
Not as I would have it,
Trusting that You will make all things right,
If I surrender to Your will,
So that I may be reasonably happy in this life,
And supremely happy with You forever in the next.

Amen.

Show me your ways, LORD, teach me your paths. Guide me in
your truth and teach me, for you are God my Savior, and my hope
is in you all day long. ~Psalm 25:4-5

The Prayer to Our Father
(translated from Aramaic)

Oh Thou, from whom the breath of life comes,
who fills all realms of sound, light and vibration.
May Your light be experienced in my utmost holiest.
Your Heavenly Domain approaches.
Let Your will come true - in the universe (all that vibrates)
just as on earth (that is material and dense).
Give us wisdom (understanding, assistance) for our daily need,
detach the fetters of faults that bind us, (karma)
like we let go the guilt of others.
Let us not be lost in superficial things (materialism, common
temptations),
but let us be freed from that what keeps us off from our true
purpose.
From You comes the all-working will, the lively strength to act,
the song that beautifies all and renews itself from age to age.

Amên. Sealed in trust, faith and truth.
(I confirm with my entire being)

A Primary School's version of The Lord's Prayer (I love this!)

Our Father in heaven, you are awesome! Show us who you are and
how you want us to be. Make earth more like heaven. Please give
us what we need to keep going each day. Help us when we are
wrong and clean us up on the inside. Help us to let other people off
and move on. Keep us from bad stuff. You're in charge! You're
strong and powerful and always there. Forever! Amen.

Prayer of Surrender to the Flower of Heaven

The following prayer is a beautiful prayer of surrender. It may move and transform your very life. Feel free to embody it as it is, or adapt it to reflect your connection and needs. If you feel inspired, it can become a daily prayer or a commitment to shine the best of you to bless your life, family, friends, and the world.

Dear Divine Creator of All, May the Grace of Love awaken all aspects of me. I choose to be a Divine blessing to the world. Forgive me for any and all suffering that I have created for anyone in this lifetime or any other lifetime. Please forgive me. And forgive me for any and all suffering that I have created for myself in this lifetime or any other lifetime.

I choose to surrender to You all that does not serve my highest good and greatest joy. I choose to surrender to all that is for my highest good and greatest joy.

I choose Love, Peace and Harmony. I choose to surrender to the Flower of Heaven and invite the Flower of Heaven to blossom in my heart center.

Let me be the gift of loving friendship to the world. May Divine Wisdom, Unconditional Love, and Grace move through, around and radiate out from me.

Guide the soul that I am, this mind and body in every interaction I share with another person. Awaken the best of me, the Truth of me, so I may serve my brothers and sisters in the world.

Amen Aum ॐ   آمِين   אָ.מ.ן   ἀμήν   ኣሜን

Metta Friendship Prayer

Another powerful prayer mantra is Metta practice. Metta is a Buddhist practice of loving kindness that originated from ancient Vedic traditions. There are many variations, but the premise is the same: a heartfelt prayer or mantra for the happiness of all beings. It is a simple yet powerful prayer that assists the practitioner to open their heart center and to develop compassion and equanimity. To begin, focus on yourself, then loved ones, people you feel neutral to, people you are challenged by, and finally all sentient beings. True kindness and compassion liberate the heart!

I first learned about the Metta practice at age 23 when I was suffering from anxiety and PTSD in university. I met a man who changed the course of my life with his compassionate presence and his sage advice. I only met him once, but I consider him a true friend. My psychic abilities began to develop when I was thirteen, and each night for ten years after, I saw dark energies that kept me awake and afraid. Out of fear of being labelled crazy, he was only the second person I shared my story of suffering with. I feel grateful I trusted him that day, as he reoriented my mind to perceive my circumstances differently and changed the course of my life.

He said, "My dear, you are experiencing a spiritual awakening. What if what you are experiencing is a type of training? These entities cannot hurt you; they can only make you think they can hurt you. They come to you because you can see them. Use the gift of your sight and knowing that they cannot hurt you to free them and yourself."

I had never contemplated this before. His question opened me deeply. I moved from a fear state to a curious state. Then he gave me a Metta practice to do for myself, these entities, and the world. He said to apply the practice anytime I felt angry, scared, or thought I was being influenced. I used it and felt a shift within my physiology, mindset, energy, and consciousness. Practicing loving kindness moved me from a state of disempowerment into an experience of empowerment.

For those with anxiety, the fears that the mind reminds you of are like these entities. The fears cannot hurt you; the mind can only trick you into believing they can. When you believe the fears, you spiral into deeper anxiety and you often create the circumstances you fear. Begin to shine the light of Truth upon the lies of the mind. Choose to know you are safe. Choose to be free of the ideas that cause you harm. Read the *Freedom from Influence* exercise in Chapter 8 to learn more.

Metta Prayer Instructions

Once you learn Metta you can do Metta practice anywhere: while driving, sitting, laying on a beach, or walking in the forest. To establish a practice, commit to at least ten minutes a day for a week and see how you feel. You can always do longer sessions when you have more time and feel more familiar with the practice.

Beginning by sitting or lying in a relaxed and comfortable position, in a quiet area, is often most effective because you can let go of other distractions or concerns.

Take a few minutes to feel the breath slowly filling your lungs and moving through the heart chakra at the center of your chest. Allow yourself to experience long, full exhalations.

Begin by slowly repeating:

May I be filled with loving kindness. May I be safe and protected. May I be well. May I live joyfully. May I be peaceful and at ease.

Allow yourself to feel and express loving intentions for yourself. Feel and see yourself filled with loving kindness, wellness, joy, peace, and ease. To assist yourself you may want to envision yourself as a new-born baby, or even as you are today. Envision yourself filled with loving, golden light or whatever colors represent love to you.

After cultivating loving-kindness toward yourself, think of a friend or family member who has deeply cared for you and whom you deeply care for. Then slowly repeat the prayer:

May you be filled with loving kindness.
May you be safe and protected.
May you be well. May you live joyfully.
May you be peaceful and at ease.

Allow yourself to rest into your intention for them. With each phrase feel and envision them being filled with loving kindness, wellness, joy, peace, and ease. Allow any feelings of compassion or loving kindness to arise within you.

Next, repeat the prayer for people you feel neutral to: neighbors, animals, communities, people who challenge or irritate you, and Mother earth.

May you be filled with loving kindness.
May you be safe and protected.
May you be well. May you live joyfully.
May you be peaceful and at ease.

Then repeat the prayer for all sentient beings:

May all beings be filled with loving kindness.
May all beings be safe and protected.
May all beings be well.
May all beings live joyfully.
May all beings be peaceful and at ease.

Imagine all forms of life in the Universe being blessed by your loving kindness prayer. See them being filled with loving kindness and feeling safe, well, joyful, peaceful, and at ease. Allow yourself to feel a deep sense of unity or loving interconnectedness with everyone and everything.

During your practice, if sadness, anger, frustration, or grief come up, direct loving kindness to those parts of you that are experiencing those states, or direct loving kindness to the emotions themselves.

Calling in a Friend

A few years ago, I was contemplating the lack of deep friendships with females. I had beautiful friendships with men. I felt ready to have a new, deep friendship with a woman. I prayed, *"I am ready and I choose a loving, conscious woman who has a child either a little older than my son or a little younger than my son. She has excellent parenting skills and shares a similar mindset around diet."*

A couple of weeks later a beautiful friend came into my life. I met her outside of a gymnastics class our children shared together. Our kids were the last two to leave the room and the instructor said, "These two are so intelligent. I was teaching the class about the benefits of fish oil and they knew all about how it helped the brain."

We turned to each other and she asked, "What kind of fish oil do you give your son?" It was love at first shared understanding. We made plans to have a playdate. She had two children. One was a little older than my son and the other was a little younger than my son. We shared common beliefs about parenting and diet. How is that for a specific prayer being answered?!

A couple of months later my friend shared with me, "You know, I manifested you into my life?" I enthusiastically blurted out, "No, I manifested you into my life!" As it goes, she had made a similar prayer at the same time I had.

If you are ready for deep friendships with your existing friends or with new ones, proclaim a declaration, set an intention, or make a clear prayer.

Attracting a New Friend

Use statements that begin with "*I choose* ...." Be specific about the type of friend you would like to attract. Trust that there is someone else who is looking for a friend like you. Let the two of you draw each other near. Who knows when or where you will meet that friend.

Strengthening Existing Friendships

For existing friends and family you might declare:

I choose to share the joys and freedom of life with loving friends.
I choose to love and accept my friends and family just as they are.
I choose peace when interacting with others.
I choose to communicate peacefully.

Powerful Afformations

Many people are familiar with *affirmations*, which are positive statements made to convince the mind of something else you would like to embody. They sound nice and can work for some people over a very long period of time. However, the subconscious mind can often block these statements, and even reinforce the negative, if they are not in alignment with what it has experienced.

Afformations, on the other hand, are very powerful and create more rapid and lasting change for people. Afformations are positive questions that bypass the gatekeeping subconscious mind. This occurs because the mind accepts what it believes is true. If you say, "I attract wealth and success," and it is not true, the mind will say, "That's not true."

If you say, "Why is it so joyful to attract wealth and success?" the mind cannot deny this statement, because it would be joyful. So, the subconscious mind accepts the question and then goes to work to answer it. So, the response is more like, "I don't know, let me find out why it is so joyful to attract wealth and success." You do not need to answer the question, you move on and let your subconscious mind answer the question in its own timing. As it looks for the answers, it attracts what it is focusing on into your life.

One at a time, compare how you feel when you speak these two statements out loud:

Affirmation
"I attract loving and supportive people into my life."

Afformation
"Why is it so joyful to attract loving and supportive people into my life?"

To cultivate or attract loving friendships ask:

- Why is it so joyful to love others and accept others unconditionally?
- Why is it so peaceful to accept myself and others as they are?
- Why is it so empowering to love the world as it is?
- Why is it so freeing to love the world as it is?
- Why do I feel so radiant loving the world as it is?
- Why is it so easy to attract loving, supportive and fun friends?
- Why do I feel so joyful opening my heart to my family and friends?
- Why is it so empowering to feel relaxed when I meet new people?
- Why is it so joyful to feel relaxed at social events?
- Why is it so connecting to get out into the social world?
- Why is it so satisfying to connect with others?

Chapter 12
Flower of Heaven Guided Meditation

Meditation in general is helpful for relaxing the mind and body. There are many types of meditation to achieve a variety of results. The Flower of Heaven meditation is a guided meditation designed to open you deeper to Love.

The Flower of Heaven meditation suggests using the Lotus Mudra. Some consider mudras merely a symbolic gesture. However, when applied correctly, mudras can be powerful hand, finger, or body positions that open the flow of energy in the body and expand consciousness.

However, you do not have to use this mudra during this meditation. If you feel more relaxed to have your hands resting, feel free to let them be where they are most comfortable.

There are various types of mudras for anything from meditation, tantra, consciousness expansion, and body healing mudras. When one is in an elevated conscious state, mudras can spontaneously occur.

The Lotus Mudra is a lovely mudra of surrender that is practiced to activate and open the heart chakra (heart center) to cultivate loving compassion toward others, to purify the heart center, and to open you to love, joy, and peace.

The lotus flower is a sacred symbol of awakening in the light of Truth after emerging from the darkness of illusion. The lotus flower is well known as an iconic symbol in Hinduism, Buddhism, ancient Egyptian traditions, and is now often associated with spirituality in the West. The symbolic use of the Lotus Mudra is a powerful reminder of the process of awakening from darkness to light.

Meditation Instructions

Download the free MP3 for the meditation at: https://www.tarabianca.com/FoH-guided-meditation

Here is a diagram of the hand position for the Lotus Mudra for later in the meditation:

Choose a comfortable position for your body: sitting cross-legged, laying down, sitting upright in a chair, or standing with your legs just slightly apart. Keep your tongue lightly on the roof of your mouth. Begin playing the guided meditation, your eyes can be

closed or open, whatever is safe and relaxing, and I will guide you with my voice.

If you are unable to download the meditation or would prefer to do it through your own guidance, here are written instructions for the Flower of Heaven Meditation that are similar to my version. It will give you a framework to create your own meditation.

Written Instructions

In a comfortable position, with your hands resting wherever they feel most relaxed, take a nourishing breath in and out. Let every breath you breathe take you deeper and deeper into relaxation.

For a moment, become aware of your heart centre, which is located at nipple level in the centre of your breastbone.

Connect from the heart with the Divine, by imagining a connection of Love between your heart centre and the heart of the Divine. It could be a river of purple light, a golden cord, or a silver thread. Whatever that looks like to your imagination, let it be.

Then say:

Dear God/Universe/Love/Christ/Allah/Creator …. I love you. Thank you, thank you, thank you for the blessings of this day. Please forgive me for any and all suffering that I have created for myself or anyone else in this lifetime or any other lifetime. Guide me to learn from my mistakes and to open the Truth of who I am. Reveal to me all the ways that I can open to Love and Peace.

Now, become aware of your crown chakra, which is located at the top of your head. Imagine glowing golden Divine Light above your head.

Say:

I choose to receive and be blessed by Divine Light. I choose for Divine Light to permeate my whole beingness. I choose to be a channel of pure Light. May the Wisdom of Divine Light heal, nourish, purify, protect, and bless me for my highest good and greatest joy, and for the highest good and greatest joy of humanity. Thank you, thank you, thank you.

Now see beautiful glowing, vibrating Divine Light, like a vortex of spiraling energy. Smile to that energy. The bottom of the vortex of Light begins to enter in through the top of your head and the vortex of healing energy slowly moves through your head and down through the centre of your body. The healing, pulsing light disperses to the tips of your fingers and all the way down to the tips of your toes. See your whole body filled with golden Divine Light.

See that Light expand out from your body into your energy field, so that you are surrounded with glowing Divine Light, much like you are inside an eggshell of light.

Take a moment to acknowledge you are a channel of Light and feel the blessing of being nourished by Divine Light.

Place your hands in the Lotus Mudra position at the level of your heart centre.

Set your intention to receive the Flower of Heaven into your heart centre by saying:

Teach me dear Highest God. I choose to surrender to Divine Truth. Guide and teach me to surrender to Unconditional Love and Holy Friendship. I choose to receive your mentorship. I choose to be the embodiment of Divine Love, Wisdom and Truth. I choose the Flower of Heaven within me. Whatever I experience, let it be for all humanity. Thank you, thank you, thank you.

Envision your heart centre full of all that you choose to embody. See and feel the Wisdom of the Flower of Heaven blooming there.

See the vibrant and magnificent colors of the Flower of Heaven shining loving acceptance out to the world. The petals sparkle with radiant aliveness and shine with Unconditional Love. See its fragrance, like smoky diffused soft light, intelligently float out from you on, blessing everyone you encounter. Then say:

Dear Divine Flower of Heaven,
May I remember Love in all my interactions. Let loving, peaceful awareness guide my heart in all that I say, do, and think toward myself and toward others.

May the Grace of Love bless my life in all ways. Guide me to be a loving and grateful friend to all people, the Holy Earth that is our home, and all of God's creation.

When faced with the sorrow, confusion, anger, or violence of others, strengthen me to stay in the power of me, free to shine with unconditional loving friendship.

Let me be in the power of who I truly AM, so that I may receive the guidance of the Divine Truth and Wisdom when others are challenged by unresolved emotional conflicts. Let me remember my brothers and sisters always in Love, even when they are lost in the illusion.

May my friends and family be remembered in Love.
May my friends and family know love, peace, and joy.
May my brothers and sisters around the world know love, peace, and joy.

May the Divine creation of the Earth and the Universe embody love, peace, and joy.

Thank you, thank you, thank you. Amen / Om

Then finish your meditation with your hands resting in your lap and allow yourself to feel the peace of blessings you have chosen. When you are ready, open your eyes and take a relaxing breath.

Conclusion

The Flower of Heaven, which is the blessing of friendship, is about actively cultivating connection through lovingly serving the world. I share the blessing of this message, as it has been serving me most of my life. However, I have gone into a new level that has awakened a fiercely joyful power within my heart for you. Join me in this beautiful song of loving the world.

Let the Lord of the Dance, the Creator of Existence, the Lover of All, the Servant of Creation, the Acceptor of All, the Singer of Everythingness beckon you into a Divine romance with your friends, family, and the world. Let this invitation be a vehicle for profound personal healing and spiritual growth.

If you would like to share the joy of this message with a friend, or if you know someone who is struggling who would feel uplifted and benefit from this message, please send them *The Flower of Heaven* book. I appreciate you sharing this message with the world.

May the words of The Great Master, Jesus the Christ, summarize the teachings of the Flower of Heaven, as he was the most loving mentor to have shared the Flower of Heaven.

There is an important concept to hold in your awareness, whether you are familiar with the Christian bible or not. Typically, when Jesus gives a commandment, Christians hear this as a rule to follow. However, commandments are actually more like blessings. Jesus commands the following as a guided invitation to attain a particular result, but also as a type of powerful blessing that activates, compels and ensures that you receive the blessing. All it takes is surrender and receptivity.

"As the Father has loved me, so have I loved you. Abide in my love. If you keep my commandments, you will abide in my love, just as I have kept my Father's commandments and abide in his love. These things I have spoken to you, that my joy may be in you, and that your joy may be full.

This is my commandment, that you love one another as I have loved you. Greater love has no one than this, that someone lay down his life for his friends. You are my friends if you do what I command you. No longer do I call you servants, for the servant does not know what his master is doing; but I have called you friends, for all that I have heard from my Father I have made known to you. You did not choose me, but I chose you and appointed you that you should go and bear fruit and that your fruit should abide, so that whatever you ask the Father in my name, he may give it to you. These things I command you, so that you will love one another." ~ John 15:9-17

I wish you every bright blessing for a joy-filled life. You are my friend in creation and in the Divine Love of God.

Love, Tara

Acknowledgements

With deep gratitude I thank everyone who has ever touched my life. Thank you, God, dearest Divine, for inspiring me to be curious and ask questions, play hide n' seek with you, investigate the mystery, accept and love others unconditionally, see the incredible beauty of life, honor the beauty of each person I meet, and receive the blessings of the Flower of Heaven. What an amazing blessing it is to lovingly serve you and your children!

To the Holy Mother for your loving embrace, unconditional love, and mentorship. To Christ for showing me the Way to Love.

To the spiritual Masters and Saints who make it possible for all of us to heal and open our hearts to Truth, Love, Wisdom and Grace, thank you sincerely.

To all of Nature, for your friendship and service.

I am grateful for all my teachers, both seen and unseen, for your service, love, and mentorship. To Master Peter Hudoba for embodying pure love of the Divine Mother. To Master Vimal for your guidance to be free of influence. To Lynne Gordon-Mündel for teaching me the simple and powerful blessing of presence.

To the Yawanawa and all the guardians of the Amazon forest, thank you for safeguarding the Holy Garden on behalf of me and everyone. Thank you for inviting me into a field of Love and sharing your home. I am honored by your service to humanity and the Divine.

To all love activists - past, present, and future - thank you for actively demonstrating love for your sisters and brothers, the earth and the Divine.

To my beautiful friends and family, thank you. To my Dad who saw my potential and taught me equality, stick-to-it-ness, discipline, and to take care of what needs to be done. You trained me well. And you surprised me with your Love Wisdom that day we walked on the beach.

To my Mom for birthing me, caring for me, and having the wisdom to ask God to look after and guide me throughout my life: a beautiful gift! To my sister Jenny for your caring heart. To my sister Kelly for supporting me in my roughest times.

To Kai, oh sweet Kai, you are an incredible teacher. How lucky that we chose each other!

To Joan for your loving friendship and inspiring mentorship as a love activist. Your faith and devotion to God is lovely.

To Paulo for shepherding a field of light for the Flower of Heaven to be revealed.

To Devyn for your receptivity and enthusiasm for Love, Truth & Freedom. It is an honor to work alongside of you. Thank you for all that you do.

To James for your unwavering friendship and loving support. You delight me, sir! Thank you for your beautiful edits and contributions to this book.

To Tim for your devotion to God. I appreciate your thoughtful and invaluable edits, comments, and contributions. Your friendship, counsel, and clarity are refreshing.

To Christine for your friendship, celebration, encouragement, and for being my most earnest fan.

To Tanya for your passionate and helpful edits for this book.

To Titus for being an inspiration for many of the sections of this book. I deeply appreciate how your presence in my life has revealed so many mysteries and strengthened my faith in God.

To Nazli, thank you for reminding me of community and friendship. You are a blessing, dear sister!

To Patricia, thank you for your suggestions and encouragement.

About the Author

Tara is a love activist, spiritual mentor, speaker, and leader in transformation.

She combines over 20 years of research, teaching, speaking, and private coaching experience with expertise in healing the mind, body, and soul to help people revolutionize their life for success.

Her multidisciplinary approach guides people through quantum shifts to access their ability to create a life from an entirely different level of consciousness. She inspires them to be a source of inspiration for others in the world and to awaken their Divine Heart to embody presence and unconditional love.

Tara is known for her compassionate, unconditionally loving heart. She knows the Divinity of each person she encounters. Tara frees them to explore life as they choose for themselves, while she invites them to choose to experience their own Divine beauty.

Tara's clients have included athletes, professionals, entrepreneurs, creatives, couples, expecting parents, children and Academy Award-nominated actors.

She writes and teaches about love, transformation, spirituality, consciousness, stress management, health & wellness, biohacking, neurohacking, nutrition, relationships, parenting, and pregnancy.

Tara lives between ocean and rainforest in beautiful Vancouver, BC, Canada.

Sources

[1] Exodus 3:14

[2] Romans 11:36

[3] Luke 17:21

[4] John 14:6

[5] Tao de Ching

[6] Mundaka Upanishad 3:1:2-3

[7] Vanier, Jean, "Transforming Our Hearts." (speech March 11, 2015), Templeton Prize News Conference, British Academy, London, March 11, 2015, https://www.mercatornet.com/articles/view/transforming-our-hearts-the-larche-answer-to-a-world-crisis/15827

[8] Dan L. *The Works of Lao Tzyy Truth and Nature.* The World Book Company, Ltd. Taipei, Taiwan, China. Ch.34, p.17, 1969.

[9] Matthew 25:40

[10] Mark 9:35-37

[11] Mark 9:42

[12] Luke 18:17

[13] Hunt, Tam. "Could consciousness all come down to the way things vibrate?" The Conversation. 9 Nov 2018 https://theconversation.com/could-consciousness-all-come-down-to-the-way-things-vibrate-103070

[14] "Cigna Loneliness Index Report." *Cigna*. Published May 2018. https://www.multivu.com/players/English/8294451-cigna-us-loneliness-survey/docs/IndexReport_1524069371598-173525450.pdf

[15] Marjoribanks D & Darnell-Bradley A. "The Way We Are Now – The state of the UK's relationships." 2017 March https://https://www.relate.org.uk/sites/default/files/the_way_we_are_now_-_youre_not_alone.pdf

[16] DiJulio B, Hamel L, Munana C & Brodie M. "Loneliness and Social Isolation in the United States, the United Kingdom, and Japan: An international Survey." *Kaiser Family Foundation*. Published August 2018. http://files.kff.org/attachment/Report-Loneliness-and-Social-Isolation-in-the-United-States-the-United-Kingdom-and-Japan-An-International-Survey.

[17] Beth. "30% Of Single Japanese Men Have Never Dated A Woman." Japan Crush. 3 Apr 2013. https://www.japancrush.com/2013/stories/30-of-single-japanese-men-have-never-dated-a-woman.html

[18] Haworth, Abigail. *The Guardian*. 20 Oct 2013. https://www.theguardian.com/world/2013/oct/20/young-people-japan-stopped-having-sex

[19] Holt-Lunstad J, Smith TB, et al. "Loneliness and Social Isolation as Risk Factors for Mortality: A Meta-Analytic Review." *Perspectives on Psychological Science*, 2015; 10 (2): 227 DOI: 10.1177/1745691614568352

[20] Cole SW, Hawkley L, et al. "Social regulation of gene expression in humans: Glucocorticoid resistance in the leukocyte transcriptome." *Genome Biol*. 2007 (8).

[21] Jaremka LM, Fagundes CP, et al. "Loneliness promotes inflammation during acute stress." *Psychol Sci* 2013; 24:1089–1097. 10.1177/0956797612464059

[22] Donovan NJ, Wu Q, et al. "Loneliness, depression and cognitive function in older U.S. adults." *Int J Geriatr Psychiatry*. 2016 May 09; doi: 10.1002/gps.4495.

[23] Lai JCL, Chong AML, et al. "Social Network Characteristics and Salivary Cortisol in Healthy Older People." *The Scientific World Journal*, vol. 2012, Article ID 929067, 8 pages, 2012. https://doi.org/10.1100/2012/929067.

[24] Ho CY. "Better Health with More Friends: The Role of Social Capital in Producing Health." *Health Econ.* 2016 Jan; 25(1): 91-100. doi: 10.1002/hec.3131. Epub 2014 Nov 27.

[25] Amati V, Meggiolaro S, Rivellini G and Zaccarin S. "Social Relations and Life Satisfaction: The Role of Friends." Genus. 2018; 54(1): 7. Published online 2018 May 4. doi: 10.1186/s41118-018-0032-z

[26] Shin SY, Lee SG. "Effects of Hospital Workers' Friendship Networks on Job Stress." *PLos One.* 2016; 11(2): e0149428. Published online 2016 Feb 22. doi: 10.1371/journal.pone.0149428

[27] Rowland L, Curry OS. "A range of kindness activities boost happiness." *J Soc Psychol.* 2019; 159(3):340-343. doi: 10.1080/00224545.2018.1469461. Epub 2018 May 15.

[28] Davidson JE, Graham P, et al. "Code Lavender: Cultivating Intentional Acts of Kindness in Response to Stressful Work Situations." *Explore (NY).* 2017 May - Jun; 13 (3):181-185. doi: 10.1016/j.explore.2017.02.005. Epub 2017 Apr 12.

[29] Chancellor J, Margolis S, et al. "Everyday prosociality in the workplace: The reinforcing benefits of giving, getting, and glimpsing." *Emotion.* 2018 Jun; 18(4):507-517. doi: 10.1037/emo0000321. Epub 2017 Jun 5.

[30] Schacter HL, Margolin G. "When it feels good to give: Depressive symptoms, daily prosocial behavior, and adolescent mood." *Emotion.* 2018 Aug 23. doi: 10.1037/emo0000494.

[31] Karen, Robert. Becoming Attached: First Relationships and How They Shape Our Capacity to Love. New York: Oxford University Press, 1994.

[32] Doré BP, Morris RR, et al. "Helping Others Regulate Emotion Predicts Increased Regulation of One's Own Emotions and Decreased Symptoms of Depression." *Pers Soc Psychol Bull.* 2017 May; 43(5):729-739. doi: 10.1177/0146167217695558. Epub 2017 Mar 20.

[33] Fischer A, Hess U. "Mimicking emotions." *Curr Opin Psychol.* 2017 Oct; 17:151-155. doi: 10.1016/j.copsyc.2017.07.008. Epub 2017 Jul 15.

[34] Becker ES, Götz T, et al. "The importance of teachers' emotions and instructional behavior for their students' emotions – An experience sampling analysis." *Teaching and Teacher Education* 2014, 43:15-26. DOI: https://doi.org/10.1016/j.tate.2014.05.002

[35] Howes MJ, Hokanson JE, Lowenstein DA. "Induction of depressive affect after prolonged exposure to a mildly depressed individual." *J Pers Soc Psychol.* 1985; 49: 1110-3.

[36] Kramer, AD, Guillory JE and Hancock JT. "Experimental evidence of massive-scale emotional contagion through social networks." PNAS. 17 June 2014 111 (24) 8788-8790; first published June 2, 2014 https://doi.org/10.1073/pnas.1320040111

[37] Eisenberg D, Golberstein E, et al. "Social contagion of mental health: evidence from college roommates." *Health Econ.* 2013 Aug; 22(8):965-86. doi: 10.1002/hec.2873. Epub 2012 Oct 11.

[38] Buchanan TW, Bagley SL, et al. "The empathic, physiological resonance of stress." *Soc Neurosci.* 2012; 7(2):191-201. doi: 10.1080/17470919.2011.588723. Epub 2011 Jul 21.

[39] Morris, Steve. "Achieving Collective Coherence: Group Effects on Heart Rate Variability Coherence and Heart Rhythm Synchronization." *Alternative Therapies*, 2010 jul/aug, VOL. 16, NO. 4. https://www.heartmath.org/assets/uploads/2015/01/achieving-collective-coherence.pdf

[40] Worm B, Barbier E, et al. "Impacts of Biodiversity Loss on Ocean Ecosystem Services." *Science.* 2006 Nov 3: Vol. 314, Issue 5800, pp. 787-790. DOI: 10.1126/science.1132294

[41] Yazdani M, Esmaeilzadeh M, et al. "The effect of laughter Yoga on general health among nursing students." *Iran J Nurs Midwifery Res.* 2014 Jan-Feb; 19(1): 36–40.

[42] Park, Alice. "A Primer for Pessimists." *Time.* Published online 26 Mar 2009. http://content.time.com/time/magazine/article/0,9171,1887872-1,00.html

[43] Dweck, Carol. *Mindset: The New Psychology of Success.* New York: Penguin Random House, 2006.

[44] B Corps. "Declaration of Interdependence." Accessed 30 Sept 2019. https://bcorporation.net/about-b-corps

[45] Seligman ME, Steen TA, Park N, Peterson C. "Positive psychology progress: empirical validation of interventions." *Am Psychol.* 2005 Jul-Aug; 60(5): 410-21. https://www.ncbi.nlm.nih.gov/pubmed/16045394

[46] Layous K, et al. "The proximal experience of gratitude." *PLOS.* Published online 2017 Jul 7. doi: 10.1371/journal.pone.0179123

[47] Barak Y. "The immune system and happiness." *Autoimmun Rev.* 2006 Oct; 5(8):523-7. Epub 2006 Mar 21 https://www.ncbi.nlm.nih.gov/pubmed/17027886

[48] Ng MY, Wong WS. "The differential effects of gratitude and sleep on psychological distress in patients with chronic pain." *J Health Psychol.* 2013 Feb; 18 (2):263-71. doi: 10.1177/1359105312439733. Epub 2012 Mar 12. https://www.ncbi.nlm.nih.gov/pubmed/22412082

[49] Roszak Burton L. "The Neuroscience of Gratitude: What you need to know about the new neural knowledge." https://www.whartonhealthcare.org/ the_neuroscience_of_gratitude Accessed 15 May 2019

[50] Psalm 118:24

[51] Bieber, Justin. *Instagram.* 2 August 2017 at 4:45pm. https://www.instagram.com/justinbieber.

52 Frostedottir AD and Dorjee D. "Effects of Mindfulness Based Cognitive Therapy (MBCT) and Compassion Focused Therapy (CFT) on Symptom Change, Mindfulness, Self-Compassion, and Rumination in Clients with Depression, Anxiety, and Stress." Front. Psychol., 17 May 2019. https://doi.org/10.3389/fpsyg.2019.01099.

Manufactured by Amazon.ca
Bolton, ON

17703978R00136